NEW DIRECTIONS FOR ADULT AND CONTINUING EDUCATION

Susan Imel, *Ohio State University*
EDITOR-IN-CHIEF

Learning and Sociocultural Contexts

Implications for Adults, Community, and Workplace Education

Mary V. Alfred
University of Wisconsin-Milwaukee

EDITOR

Number 96, Winter 2002

JOSSEY-BASS
San Francisco

LEARNING AND SOCIOCULTURAL CONTEXTS: IMPLICATIONS FOR ADULTS,
COMMUNITY, AND WORKPLACE EDUCATION
Mary V. Alfred (ed.)
New Directions for Adult and Continuing Education, no. 96
Susan Imel, Editor-in-Chief

Microfilm copies of issues and articles are available in 16mm and 35mm,
as well as microfiche in 105mm, through University Microfilms Inc., 300
North Zeeb Road, Ann Arbor, Michigan 48106-1346.

ISSN 1052-2891   electronic ISSN 1536-0717

NEW DIRECTIONS FOR ADULT AND CONTINUING EDUCATION is part of The
Jossey-Bass Higher and Adult Education Series and is published quarterly
by Wiley Subscription Services, Inc., a Wiley company, at Jossey-Bass, 989
Market Street, San Francisco, California 94103-1741. Periodicals postage
paid at San Francisco, California, and at additional mailing offices. Postmaster: Send address changes to New Directions for Adult and Continuing Education, Jossey-Bass, 989 Market Street, San Francisco, California,
94103-1741.

SUBSCRIPTIONS cost $70.00 for individuals and $149.00 for institutions,
agencies, and libraries.

EDITORIAL CORRESPONDENCE should be sent to the Editor-in-Chief, Susan
Imel, ERIC/ACVE, 1900 Kenny Road, Columbus, Ohio 43210-1090.
e-mail: imel.l@osu.edu.

Cover photograph by Wernher Krutein/PHOTOVAULT © 1990.

www.josseybass.com

Printed in the United States of America on acid-free recycled paper con-
taining at least 20 percent postconsumer waste.

CONTENTS

EDITOR'S NOTES

Although adults have long faced the personal experience of learning in many social and cultural contexts, little is understood about the process of learning in these various contexts. Learning is viewed as a personal process, but it is the perspective of the authors in this volume that social and cultural contexts shape what an adult needs and wants to learn, when and where the learning takes place, and how the learning is perceived.

In this volume of *New Directions for Adult and Continuing Education,* we explore some of the contexts within which learning occurs and the social and cultural dynamics that influence learning and teaching. It is important to note that because context is fluid and forever changing, it is not possible to address the multitude of contexts relative to learning and teaching. Our aim is to create awareness of the importance of context in adult learning and to encourage adult educators to be reflective on their practice, to understand how social and cultural contexts influence classroom dynamics, and to take critical action to ameliorate hegemonic practices in adult education. Therefore, in Chapter One, I critique the individualistic perspective as being the most dominant philosophy guiding current practices of adult education and recommend sociocultural theory as a promising framework for moving the field to a more democratic position.

In the next three chapters, the authors use examples from their lived experience to demonstrate the influence of sociocultural context in adult learning. In Chapter Two, Juanita Johnson-Bailey, an African American female, and Ronald Cervero, a white male, document their personal experience of learning in a cross-cultural mentoring relationship and highlight the contextual issues that influence development and maintenance of such a learning relationship.

In Chapter Three, Ming-Yeh Lee and Vanessa Sheared explore the influence of formal and informal socialization as context for learning. Drawing from Ming-Yeh's experiences as an Asian immigrant in U.S. adult education, the authors explore the cultural and social norms and practices that facilitate and inhibit learning among foreign-born students.

Similarly, technology-enhanced courses on the Internet are an increasingly popular delivery option throughout formal systems of adult higher education. In Chapter Four, Simone Conceição draws from her experience as a foreign-born learner, learning within the context of cyberspace. She shows how learning from that context created a safe space for constructing knowledge that helped transform her early conceptualization of learning and teaching.

In the next four chapters, the authors explore the concept of learning in more traditional settings and show how adult educators must pay attention to those contextual issues that shape adult learning experiences. For example, research on adult learners with disabilities has primarily emphasized services related to literacy intervention, program offerings, and accommodation, thus treating learners as a monolithic group. In Chapter Five, Jovita Ross-Gordon shows how the sociocultural contexts of race, class, and gender influence the learning experience of adults with disabilities and offers implications for providing services for a culturally diverse group of learners with disabilities.

Similarly, there are many reasons learners participate in community-sponsored adult basic education programs. These various motivational factors, coupled with the cultural and ethnic diversity among learners in literacy programs, bring myriad cultural values and expectations to the ABE classroom. Yet the dominant adult literacy education model continues to take a uniform, one-size-fits-all approach. In Chapter Six, Barbara Sparks argues for a more sociocultural approach to literacy education, one that takes into account the various ways by which literacy is acquired and used in social interactions and situational contexts.

From the perspective of workplace learning, changing demographics bring new challenges for organizations and participants to meet the need for a competent workforce. In Chapter Seven, Laura Bierema explores how the changing demographics of today's workforce (for example, the increase in older workers, cultural and ethnic minorities, and non-English-speaking immigrants) shape the sociocultural dynamics of learning in the workplace.

Additionally, as working life becomes more professionalized, practitioners are mandated with the task of participating in continuing education activities to maintain and regulate their practice. In Chapter Eight, Barbara Daley examines learning within professional practice and shows how the contextual characteristics of the profession frame what is learned and how that knowledge is used.

Finally, in the closing chapter, I draw from the recommendations and ideas that the authors have presented to recommend a process for moving to a more democratic adult education practice, one that incorporates the sociocultural contexts of learners' and instructors' experiences.

Mary V. Alfred
Editor

MARY V. ALFRED is assistant professor of adult and continuing education in the Department of Administrative Leadership at the University of Wisconsin-Milwaukee.

1

*The most dominant perspectives used to understand adult
learning and guide the practice of adult education
continue to be those that focus on learning as an
individual endeavor with little regard for the
sociocultural environment. Sociocultural theory therefore
holds promise for incorporating multiple worldviews into
the study and practice of adult education.*

The Promise of Sociocultural Theory in Democratizing Adult Education

Mary V. Alfred

Recent demographic trends present an astounding picture of change in the nation as a whole, and specifically in our educational institutions. According to Olson and Mullen (1990), a public school teacher from California who was teaching language arts, reading, and social studies at the middle school level made this observation about the diversity of the students in her class: "Samoan, Tongan, Hispanic students from Central America and Latin America; we have Russian children, and a lot from Fiji. Japan, of course, many from Hong Kong, Taiwan and Indonesia. Did I say Vietnamese: We have many Vietnamese, and quite a few from the Philippines. And, we have people migrating from the east coast, from the South. We have all colors and languages and nations here" (cited in Perez, 1998, p. 3).

This observation was made of an elementary school classroom, but it is not far removed from what could be said of an adult education classroom, particularly adult basic or literacy education. To these observed differences in culture, ethnicity, language, nationality, and race we can add the differences of age, gender, sexual orientation, physical ability, and socioeconomic status, to name a few. These changes in the demographic makeup of adult learners bring excitement as well as challenge to the field of adult education. The excitement comes from the opportunity for change and innovative practice that can result in an attempt to embrace the diversity of perspectives that learners bring. On the other hand, the challenging question that today's adult educators are faced with is the extent to which these diverse contexts influence learning, and how to create a responsible learning environment where students can participate in the discourse of learning without sacrificing their personal and cultural identity. In other words, how can adult educators, practicing within a Eurocentric dominant institutional culture, validate the myriad social and cultural contexts from which learners' experiences emanate? These experiences have value intrinsically; our job, it seems, is to recognize and capitalize upon that value.

Although the value of sociocultural contexts in influencing adult learning has widely been acknowledged within the field of adult education, the dominant theories of the field (for example, Knowles, 1980; Mezirow, 1991; Tough, 1971) still promote an individual or cognitive perspective of learning, which continues to privilege the Eurocentric worldview.

A Closer Look at the Individual/Cognitive View of Learning

Early cognitive theories assumed that a cognitive core of knowledge and skills exists in the mind of the individual, independent of context and intention. These theories formulated learning as acquisition of concepts and skills that can be learned independently of outside influence. According to this perspective, one facilitates learning by breaking a complex task into component parts to be taught and learned in practical isolation by the individual learner (Deci and Ryan, 1985). Those who anchor their work within the individual framework propose a clear relation among beliefs, attitudes, and values as motivational forces for learning. In other words, the extent to which one engages in an activity depends upon the beliefs one has about self-competency or efficacy, how much one values a given task, and the degree to which this value is extrinsic or intrinsic (Deci and Ryan, 1985). Those who hold this view see these individual beliefs, values, or goals for learning as critical determinants for academic success.

This perspective presents a static view of learning and fails to account for how issues of positionality influence the learner's experience in the adult education classroom. As an example, this view does not explain how the lived experiences of generation Xers, baby boomers, and veterans influence their worldviews, their learning, and their performance in the workplace. It takes little account of the transcultural experience of immigrant Americans and how early formal and informal socialization influences their learning in a new country. In addition, the individual perspective shows little consideration for the lived experiences of the disabled learner, or someone from a minority or lower socioeconomic group, or from various professional cultures, or those from myriad other sociocultural communities, and how these lived experiences influence learning.

Encouragingly, in recent years researchers and practitioners have come to believe that learning is a much more complex activity than the individual engagement it was once thought to be. Dissatisfied with overly individualistic learning concepts and frameworks, adult education scholars (Caffarella and Merriam, 1999; Fenwick, 2001; Guy, 1999; Hansman, 2001; Tisdell, 1995; Wilson, 1993) are arguing for the importance of social and cultural contexts in determining what and how we know and learn. The sociocultural approach holds promise for expanding the theory and practice of adult education, particularly in giving voice to the rich perspectives that learners and instructors bring to the learning environment.

Tenets of Sociocultural Theory

The theoretical underpinnings of the sociocultural view are drawn from Vygotskian theories of learning and development emphasizing that learning occurs within a social world (Vygotsky, 1978; Wertch, 1991). Sociocultural approaches to learning are based on "the concept that human activities take place in cultural contexts, are mediated by language and other symbolic systems, and can be best understood when investigated in their historical development" (John-Steiner and Mahn, 1996, p. 191). Learning and knowledge are therefore intertwined with the context within which they occur.

From this perspective, an educator must seek to understand the cultural worlds within which individuals have grown and developed; how individuals interpret who they are in relation to others; and how they have learned to process, interpret, and encode their worlds (Perez, 1998). Another tenet of sociocultural theory is that all learners are primary members of a defined culture with a cultural identity, and the degree to which they engage in learning is a function of this cultural identity (Perez, 1998). Therefore learning cannot be considered to be content-free or context-free, for it is always filtered through one's culture and cultural identity. It is, in other words, socially and culturally situated (Lave, 1988). This emphasis on the situated nature of learning shifts the focus on learning from the individual alone to the individual in interaction with and within a larger sociocultural context.

Context is thus central to the social construction of meaning and the understanding of the interactionist perspective that undergirds learning within a sociocultural environment. The environment, then, includes the individual in interactions with the culture, context, and community within which learning occurs. Indeed, it is from this sociocultural environment that the individual acquires the tools, symbols, resources, and strategies to manage the learning process. The remaining sections of this chapter address the critical dimensions of sociocultural theory: culture, context, and communities. Included in this discussion is the notion of power within and among discourse communities, a topic often overlooked in discussion of sociocultural theory.

Culture and Learning. According to Trice and Beyer, "human cultures emerge from people's struggles to manage uncertainties and to create some degree of order in social life" (1993, p. 1). Similarly, Trompenaars and Hampden-Turner note that "culture is the way in which a group of people solve problems and reconcile dilemmas" (1998, p. 6). Schein, on the other hand, defines culture as "a pattern of basic assumptions that the group learned as it solved its problems of external adaptation and internal integration that has worked well enough to be considered valid and, therefore, to be taught to new members as the correct way to perceive, think, and feel in relation to those problems" (1992, p. 13). Inherent in all three definitions is the notion that the culture of a group defines the rules of behavior and correct practices for group members. Cultural definition of these rules is the process by which group members are socialized and by which they acquire the resources, tools, and strategies necessary for group participation and for solving their day-to-day problems.

To further capture the essence of culture, Trice and Beyer (1993) identify six characteristics that shape these elusive phenomena. They note cultures to be collective, emotional, historical, symbolic, dynamic, and fuzzy:

1. Collective: cultures cannot be produced by an individual acting alone. They operate as individuals interact with each other. To belong to a culture, individuals must believe what others believe and do what they do. Persons who do not endorse and practice the prevailing beliefs, values, and norms often become marginalized or pushed out of the group.

2. Emotional: because cultures help to manage anxieties, they are infused with emotion as well as rational thought. People's allegiance to their beliefs, values, and cultural practices develops primarily from their emotional needs. As a consequence, members of a culture seldom question the core beliefs and values inherent in that culture.

3. Historically based: cultures cannot be divorced from their histories and they do not arise overnight. To develop a culture, people need to spend time together to interact and share with one another common uncertainties and some ways of coping with them. Therefore, a particular culture is based on the unique history of a particular group of people coping with a unique set of physical, social, political, and economic circumstances.

4. Inherently symbolic: cultures emphasize the expressive rather than the practical or technical side of human behavior. Cultural symbols facilitate communication and expression among cultural members.

5. Dynamic: although cultures are historical and persist across generations, they do not remain static. They continuously change because members may bring their own understanding and interpretation of cultural norms and expectations. These variations of interpretation, over time, become embedded in the culture as acceptable behavior.

6. Fuzzy: cultures are not monolithic, single sets of ideas, but are instead pluralistic and incorporate contradictions, ambiguities, paradoxes, and just plain confusion. Part of the fuzziness and confusion results from the interaction of multiple subcultures within an institution or organization. [Trice and Beyer, 1993, pp. 5–8.]

I embrace Trice and Beyer's notion of culture as plural, meaning that one does not represent a single culture but multiple cultures. An individual is thus not bounded by a culture but floats in and out of many cultures and is the product of the multiple realities of these cultures. As a result, culture must be understood discursively as an open text. It should be viewed not as a single doctrine but as a system of meanings. Each culture to which an individual belongs constitutes a toolkit of accepted ways of expressing and affirming beliefs, values, and norms.

Noting that cultures are collective, emotional, historically based, symbolic, dynamic, or fuzzy and that adult students bring multiple cultures into the classroom, how then can the adult educator meet the challenge of creating a culturally relevant and inclusive learning environment? Moreover, one must keep in mind that the educational institutions within which we practice are influenced by the sociopolitical values of the wider society, which are often based on Eurocentric values. Given this reality, is it possible for an adult educator to insulate practice from the wider institutional and societal hegemonic values, to create an inclusive environment for diverse learners? Can instructors truly create an inclusive learning environment without an understanding of the contexts that shape their lives and those of their students? In fact, is it even possible for an inclusive learning environment to exist at all? Rather than present simplistic answers to these complex questions, I present them for reflective purposes. As Pratt and Nesbit (2000) note, "Teaching adults is a complex, pluralistic, and moral undertaking. Yet, paradoxically, it is often regarded by scholars and practitioners alike as unproblematic. As teachers of adults, we are not usually urged to reflect critically on who we are, what we do, and why" (p. 117). Even so, this self-reflection is necessary. In other words, we must recognize the challenge that we undertake as we attempt to create learning programs that recognize the multiple contexts serving as sites for learning in and out of the adult education classroom.

Contexts as Sites for Learning. Defining *context* is like attempting to define *culture*. Both are fluid, dynamic, and forever changing. Noting the dynamic nature of context, Soldatova (1993) states that "research could be designed to hold a word or concept constant while varying the context or vice versa and the interest in the issue would be exhausted. But, contemporary studies in a variety of disciplines force us to recognize that a context, too, is dynamic, fluid and complex" (cited in John-Steiner, Panofsky, and Smith, 1994, p. 10).

According to Soldatova's assertion, context is defined by the interactional experiences of members of a social group, through the communicative process and the activities in which they engage. Sociocultural contexts, therefore, make up the total life space in which individual development takes place. It is the interaction of the individual with the environment (referring to the social context within a person's life). One's environment consists of the family; the community; the institution, to include the school and the workplace; and the wider society. Individual interactions can often be situated within one of these environmental contexts.

There is a tendency to view learning context in terms of physical location and the setting of the learning activity. Accordingly, Lave and Wenger (1991) suggest that context is often viewed as a container into which the individual is dropped. For example, the classroom as a physical location is often seen as the context for learning. However, the physical setting is just one contextual element. Other contextual factors are the history, culture, race, class, gender, sexual orientation, and physical ability of students and teachers; roles, responsibilities, and prior knowledge of participants within the learning community; the course design, including the curriculum and learning activities; the learning environment; and the history, culture, and structure of the educational institution, to name a few. Since these recurring contexts constitute the dominant cultures of a person's world, the interaction of these contextual factors influences the meaning that the learner makes of the learning process.

Of particular concern to adult education is the context of difference and how diversity constructs (race, class, gender, nationality, sexual preferences, and so on) manifest themselves in the classroom. Practices of racism, sexism, and ethnocentrism, for example, have been found to be overt and covert in the practice of adult education. Johnson-Bailey and Cervero (2000) note that the literature of adult education has placed value on Eurocentric knowledge and thought and has ignored knowledge constructed outside the discourse of whiteness. They shape their argument from a review of a fifty-five-year literature base of adult education, in which they discovered that issues of race have received minimal attention. As they note, "although race is a central location for the negotiation of power and privilege in education and in society, it has never formed the focal point of a single chapter in the entire corpus of eight handbooks" (2000, p. 201). Similarly, Tisdell (1993) found that both the overt and the hidden curricula in two higher education classes favored the experiences of white males. The curricula for these classes were found to omit racial and ethnic representation and place greater emphasis on male than on female experiences. The curriculum as a context for learning, then, carries the hidden message that male Eurocentric knowledge and thought represent valid ways of knowing and thus constitute the criteria by which all others should be judged. This hidden message can be empowering to white male students but oppressive to white women and students of color, thus influencing the learning experience of the students according to their sociocultural history.

Context goes beyond the physical to include individual, cultural, social, institutional, and historical locations and is a constitutive factor in our understanding of adult learning as social phenomena. Gee (1990), however, cautioned that we cannot fully understand context unless it is situated with the social group with which we are concerned. He refers to the social group as a "Discourse" community. As a result, an individual participates in multiple discourse communities, each with its own cultures, values, and role expectations.

Discourse Communities as Contexts for Learning. According to the sociocultural perspective, learning is embedded within discourse or social practice (Gee, 1990). The concept of discourse, as used in this volume, is broader than that used in the traditional social sciences to mean a system of thought based primarily on language use. In this sociocultural perspective, "attention is drawn not only to vocabularies of speech and writing but also to how they imply [a] whole network of social relationships and regularities. . . . Discourse is the means by which a group actively shapes and orders their relationships to the social world" (Pratt and Nesbit, 2000, p. 118). Gee (1990) argues that the knowledge one constructs and the skills and strategies acquired to deal with everyday life are more than acquisition of concepts and skills that can be learned independently of outside influence. To Gee, these concepts and skills grow from participation in a larger learning system or sociopolitical community or discourse.

There is a particular history, culture, and social identity to each specific discourse. Moreover, Perez (1998) sees discourse as an "identity kit" that encompasses ways of acting, talking, writing, and communicating a particular role that others recognize. One understands, however, that identity is not a fixed construct; it is negotiated as one moves within and across communities. As Hall (2000) notes, "Identity is not already there; rather it is a production, emergent, in process. It is situational—it shifts from context to context" (cited in Yon, 2000, p. xi). Identity is thus constantly reworked with meaning and images drawn from interaction within myriad discourse communities. Each discourse community has its own culture and recursive identity. By recursive identity I mean that members are constantly shaping and renegotiating the identity of the community. For example, in the 1970s, the discourse of adult education saw its identity embedded in the concept of andragogy, the practice of teaching adults (Knowles, 1980). This identity representation differentiated the field from pedagogy, meaning the practice of teaching children. Over time, the members of the community continued to shape the identity of the field by incorporating alternative identifiers, concepts, and theories to define and redefine the community. We continue to reflect on our identity and incorporate new perspectives, theories, and strategies into our practice. By so doing, we continue to redefine and renegotiate the identity of the field; hence my notion of recursive identity. Each discourse community continues to define and renegotiate its identity.

Understanding that cultures and identities are elusive constructs, always in flux, promises the cultivation of a more democratic adult education practice. We can fulfill this promise by dismantling the elite structure of the profession and renegotiating a more inclusive community, one that recognizes and embraces the multiple realities of learners and teachers.

However, before we can create such a community, we must acknowledge and begin to address the power dynamics, hegemonic practices, and alienation that are commonplace in any discourse community.

Power and Conflict Within and Among Discourse Communities

The underlying values of a discourse community or community of practice (Lave, 1988) shape how we think and produce knowledge and facilitate shared understanding and interaction. We must also understand that even as a discourse community facilitates learning, it may also work to constrain as it sets up boundaries, parameters, and criteria for membership, thus engendering exclusionary practice. Shifting our attention from the individual learner to the interaction of learner with the community within which the learning takes place brings neglected power issues into sharper focus. Indeed, a few adult education authors (Hansman and Wilson, 2002; Pratt and Nesbitt, 2000) are beginning to challenge the simplistic conceptualization of a discourse community as a site for learning, with frequent disregard for the influence of power in the learning community, but more work is needed.

For instance, we must recognize and grapple with the fact that a discourse community with majority members of a dominant group takes on the values and mores of that dominant group, regarding them as normal. At the same time, values and behaviors that do not mirror those of the majority are often viewed as deviant or wrong. As Nieto tells us, "The difference in perception is due more to the power of each of these groups than to any inherent goodness or rightness in the values themselves" (2000, p. 140). In other words, the fact that Eurocentric values and ways of knowing and behaving are perceived as superior to those of another minority group is due to the power of the white dominant culture and not to the superiority of the values themselves. As a result, we must acknowledge that there are no ultimate truths or validity to the values that Eurocentric ideals imply, and we must manifest this knowledge in our teaching.

Kent (1991) argues that a discourse community has no real validity because it is unable to define who or what has authority over another idea or belief within a community. He believes that the very notion of community is weak because it requires a "conceptual scheme" to define the knowledge of the community. This conceptual scheme helps the discourse community organize and create knowledge, and the members are dependent on this scheme to understand outside events and the world around them (Kent, 1991). Kent further argues that because there is no real truth or authority in a community, and all knowledge and truth are socially constructed, community members can never claim that they possess authority to which others should bow, or knowledge that others should regard as truth. He also argues that without this conceptual scheme, no discourse community can claim authority in knowledge and thought over other communities.

Although the sociocultural perspective of learning acknowledges multiple realities and the social construction of knowledge, the everyday practice of teaching and learning tend to adopt a position of ultimate truths, shaped by Eurocentric ideals. The sociocultural perspective holds promise for challenging the Eurocentric ideals that dominate the practice of adult education.

Promise of Sociocultural Theory in Building a More Democratic Practice

Scholars of adult education are beginning to question the extent to which the adult education discourse community empowers some learners and silences others, according to their race, culture, gender, nationality, physical ability, and sexual orientation, to name a few contexts (Alfred, 2001; Colin and Heaney, 2001; Guy, 1999; Johnson-Bailey and Cervero, 2000; Ross-Gordon, Martin, and Briscoe, 1990). To understand the adult education classroom as a viable site for learning, we must first explore the power dynamics that tend to give voice to some learners while silencing others. So the relevant question is, To what extent can the adult education classroom be democratic in its structure and orientation if it is to hear the multiple voices of community members? Colin and Heaney (2001) argue that it is possible to achieve democracy in adult education, but we must be watchful of the hegemonic structures and powers that constrain democratic practices within the wider institutional and societal cultures. They note that "because the practice of democracy is always circumscribed within regimes of power, democracy requires constant vigilance. Hence the challenge to create a participatory practice within the higher education classroom inevitably involves pushing the borders, anticipating and countering resistance. It is in engagement with this struggle that genuine participation and democracy are attained" (Colin and Heaney, 2001, pp. 29–30).

Colin and Heaney's assertion clearly supports Yon's position (2000) that although discourse acts upon people, people in turn rework and act upon discourse. If we view discourse as a fluid, discursive space that can be changed and negotiated, then sociocultural theory holds promise for informing a more inclusive adult education. I am suggesting that although a discourse community can be a site for power and domination, it can also foster the opportunity to challenge these hegemonic practices, thus changing the culture and values inherent in the community.

The sociocultural view pays attention to the values, practices, and resources inherent in a community and notes how they validate some and marginalize others. The larger question that the sociocultural view poses to the adult educator concerns the conditions the educator might create to allow multiple worldviews in adult education. In other words, how can we give value and credibility to multiple voices and shift the knowledge that dominates the field from an individualistic perspective to a more sociocultural one? Please note, moreover, that this proposition does not negate the value of cognitive theory or the individualistic perspective. In fact, as Rogoff (1995) points out, the sociocultural theory incorporates the individual, social, and cultural dimensions of learning. In so doing, the sociocultural perspective embraces, rather than rejects, the more traditional theories that dominate the field of adult education, while opening up a discursive space for acknowledging and supporting multiple ways of knowing.

References

Alfred, M. V. "The Politics of Knowledge and Theory Construction in Adult Education: A Critical Analysis from an Africentric Feminist Perspective." *MAACE Options,* 2001, *13* (1), 10–20.

Caffarella, R. S., and Merriam, S. B. "Perspectives on Adult Learning: Framing Our Research." In D. S. Smith (ed.), *Proceedings of the 40th Annual Adult Education Research Conference.* De Kalb: Northern Illinois University, 1999.

Colin, S.A.J., III, and Heaney, T. "Negotiating the Democratic Classroom." In C. A. Hansman and P. A. Sissel (eds.), *Understanding and Negotiating the Political Landscape of Adult Education.* New Directions for Adult and Continuing Education, no. 91. San Francisco: Jossey-Bass, 2001.

Deci, E. L., and Ryan, R. M. *Intrinsic Motivation and Self-Determination in Human Behavior.* New York: Plenum, 1985.

Fenwick, T. "Tides of Change: New Themes and Questions in Workplace Learning." In T. C. Fenwick (ed.), *Sociocultural Perspectives of Learning Through Work.* New Directions for Adult and Continuing Education, no. 92. San Francisco: Jossey-Bass, 2001.

Gee, J. P. *Social Linguistics and Literacies: Ideology in Discourses.* London: Palmer Press, 1990.

Guy, T. C. "Culture as Context for Adult Education: The Need for Culturally Relevant Adult Education." In T. C. Guy (ed.), *Providing Culturally Relevant Adult Education: A Challenge for the Twenty-First Century.* New Directions for Adult and Continuing Education, no. 82. San Francisco: Jossey-Bass, 1999.

Hall, S. "Forward." In D. A. Yon, *Elusive Culture: Schooling, Race, and Identity in Global Times.* Albany: State University of New York Press, 2000.

Hansman, C. A. "Context-Based Adult Learning." In S. Merriam (ed.), *The New Update on Adult Learning Theory.* New Directions for Adult and Continuing Education, no. 89. San Francisco: Jossey-Bass, 2001.

Hansman, C. A., and Wilson, A. L. "Situating Cognition: Knowledge and Power in Context." In J. M. Pettitt (ed.), *Proceedings of the 43rd Annual Adult Education Research Conference.* Raleigh: North Carolina State University, 2002.

Johnson-Bailey, J., and Cervero, R. "Race and Adult Education: A Critical Review of the North American Literature." In T. Sork, V. Lee-Chapman, and R. St. Clair (eds.), *Proceedings of the 41st Annual Adult Education Research Conference.* Vancouver: University of British Columbia, 2000.

John-Steiner, V., and Mahn, H. "Sociocultural Approaches to Learning and Development: A Vygotskian Framework." *Educational Psychologist,* 1996, *31,* 191–206.

John-Steiner, V., Panofsky, C. P., and Smith, L. W. *Sociocultural Approaches to Language and Literacy: An Interactionist Perspective.* Cambridge: Cambridge University Press, 1994.

Kent, T. "On the Very Idea of a Discourse Community." *College Composition and Communication,* 1991, *42,* 425–445.

Knowles, M. S. *The Modern Practice of Adult Education: From Pedagogy to Andragogy* (2nd ed.). New York: Cambridge University Press, 1980.

Lave, J. *Cognition in Practice.* Cambridge: Cambridge University Press, 1988.

Lave, J., and Wenger, E. *Situated Learning: Legitimate Peripheral Participation.* New York: Cambridge University Press, 1991.

Mezirow, J. *Transformative Dimensions of Adult Learning.* San Francisco: Jossey-Bass, 1991.

Nieto, S. *Affirming Diversity: The Sociopolitical Context of Multicultural Education.* New York: Longman, 2000.

Perez, B. *Sociocultural Contexts of Language and Literacy.* Mahwah, N.J.: Erlbaum, 1998.

Pratt, D. D., and Nesbit, T. "Discourses and Cultures of Teaching." In A. L. Wilson and E. R. Hayes (eds.), *Handbook of Adult and Continuing Education.* San Francisco: Jossey-Bass, 2000.

Rogoff, B. "Observing Sociocultural Activity in Three Planes: Participatory Appropriation, Guided Participation, and Apprenticeship." In J. Wertsch, P. del Rio, and A. Alvarez (eds.), *Sociocultural Studies of the Mind.* Cambridge: Cambridge University Press, 1995.

Ross-Gordon, J. M, Martin, L. G., and Briscoe, D. B. (eds.). *Serving Culturally Diverse Populations.* New Directions for Adult and Continuing Education, no. 48. San Francisco: Jossey-Bass, 1990.

Schein, E. H. *Organizational Culture and Leadership* (2nd Ed.). San Francisco: Jossey-Bass, 1992.

Tisdell, E. "Interlocking Systems of Power, Privilege, and Oppression in Adult Higher Education Classes." *Adult Education Quarterly,* 1993, *43* (4), 203–226.

Tisdell, E. J. *Creating Inclusive Adult Learning Environments: Insights from Multicultural Education and Feminist Pedagogy* (Information Series no. 361). Columbus, Ohio: ERIC Clearinghouse on Adult, Career, and Vocational Education, 1995.

Tough, A. *The Adult's Learning Projects: A Fresh Approach to Theory and Practice in Adult Learning.* Toronto: Ontario Institute for Studies in Education, 1971.

Trice, H. M., and Beyer, J. M. *The Cultures of Work Organization.* Upper Saddle River, N.J.: Prentice Hall, 1993. Adapted by permission of Pearson Education, Inc., Upper Saddle River, N.J.

Trompenaars, F., and Hampden-Turner, C. *Riding the Waves of Culture: Understanding Diversity in Global Business* (2nd ed.). New York: McGraw-Hill, 1998.

Vygotsky, L. S. *Mind in Society: The Development of Higher Psychological Processes.* Cambridge: Harvard University Press, 1978.

Wertch, J. V. *Voices of the Mind: A Sociohistorical Approach to Mediated Action.* Cambridge: Harvard University Press, 1991.

Wilson, A. L. "The Promise of Situated Cognition." In S. B. Merriam (ed.), *An Update on Adult Learning.* New Directions for Adult and Continuing Education, no. 57. San Francisco: Jossey-Bass, 1993.

Yon, D. A. *Elusive Culture: Schooling, Race, and Identity in Global Times.* Albany: State University of New York Press, 2000.

MARY V. ALFRED *is assistant professor of adult and continuing education in the Department of Administrative Leadership at the University of Wisconsin-Milwaukee.*

2

*Cross-cultural mentoring relationships are an important
site of struggle for learning and for power. We use the
example of one mentoring relationship to illustrate six
common issues facing people involved in these
relationships.*

Cross-Cultural Mentoring as a Context for Learning

Juanita Johnson-Bailey, Ronald M. Cervero

Mentoring across cultural boundaries is an especially delicate dance that
juxtaposes group norms and societal pressures and expectations with individual personality traits. Why would you choose to traverse such tumul-
tuous territory, and how do you survive the journey? In our own successful
mentoring relationship with each other, the answers are simple. We never
approached our sojourn with a consciousness burdened by societal dictates. Of course, there were those invisible knapsacks of privilege and dis-
enfranchisement on our backs (McIntosh, 1995), but more important there
were sincere and somewhat naïve beliefs that people are free to act beyond
cultural confines in spite of their fears. The common ground of our
working-class families, Catholic school histories, leftist political leanings,
and love of rhythm and blues lay undiscovered, but our generational
understandings of the world, as children marked and forever changed by
the civil rights struggle and the Kennedy assassination, afforded a common
basis on which to build a relationship.

We start off the chapter with individual accounts of our mentoring relationship. In the second section, we use our relationship and the literature
to illuminate common issues and strategies of a cross-cultural mentoring
relationship. Finally, we discuss implications for assembling the infrastructure of a successful cross-cultural mentoring relationship and the importance of mentoring in building a diverse and strong academy.

NEW DIRECTIONS FOR ADULT AND CONTINUING EDUCATION, no. 96, Winter 2002 © Wiley Periodicals, Inc.

Personal Stories

We wrote these individual accounts of our mentoring relationship independently of each other. This allows the reader to gain a sense of what each of us as an individual brings to the relationship.

Ron's Mentoring Narrative. Our story is one of transitions and constants, similarities and differences. At the level of formal roles, we have transitioned through four status changes: from student to teacher, from student to major professor, from assistant and associate professor to professor, and from faculty member to department head. The constant in our lives has been the mentoring and friendship roles that have sustained our fluctuating existence. Over time we have developed a close personal relationship as colleagues and friends, and we have traveled together in our family units, enjoying relationships with the other's family. We were both raised in working-class, Catholic families and have birthdays two years and four days apart; at the same time, I am a white man raised in the north and Juanita is a black woman raised in the south.

I have vivid memories of each phase of our relationship, especially how it began and where it currently stands. When I first met Juanita in 1990, she and Barbara, also a black woman, were in a class I taught. They were the only two black students in the class—and in our graduate program. They always sat together and for the most part kept to themselves, usually interacting as a team. In contrast to that tenuous beginning is my most recent and vivid memory of our relationship: a paper session we did at the Adult Education Research Conference in Vancouver, British Columbia. The topic was the "Invisible Politics of Race in Adult Education." I felt as if we were in battle together with a fairly hostile audience who disagreed with the notion that race and racism were present in our work as adult educators.

I had a lot of help in learning how to be in this relationship. My parents showed me that every person was a human being and thus deserved to be treated with dignity and respect. My own mentor, Phyllis Cunningham, and I worked together for over ten years in Chicago in exciting, though sometimes very difficult, multiracial work environments. I learned a lot about power and relationships from Phyllis. She continues to be a beacon for me in my own work as an adult educator.

For any relationship to be successful, both people must benefit. However, I tend to fully realize only the benefits that accrue to me. Of course, at the most basic level, I enjoy Juanita's intelligence, honesty, and friendship. There is no way I could quantify the significance of the insights and learning that have resulted from our work together. Indeed, I often wonder who is mentoring whom in this relationship.

Juanita's Mentoring Narrative. My first significant experience with Ron occurred in the summer of 1990, when I was in my second quarter of classes at the University of Georgia. I sat in his Curriculum and Development course in an atmosphere that I imagine is similar to that of most

Research One universities: white, competitive, and surface-friendly. Add to this setting the desegregation legacy of a southern university, and you have an uneasy armistice: a cease-fire classroom environment where the blacks sit with the blacks and the whites sit with the whites. Rarely does anyone reach across the racial divide, and even more rarely does someone reach across this chasm with a high degree of comfort and sincerity. Ron was that someone.

Our mentoring relationship did not begin that summer, but my observations and assessment of his character did begin in those weekend classes. Despite his kindness, I was cautious. I remember that my confidant (another black woman student) and I would wonder why he was so different. We wondered why he cared. I concluded that he acted the way he did because he remembered "when." You see, there are many of us in academia who wear the banner of our humble origins, or of our working-class background as a badge and proof of our understanding of the disenfranchised. Yet oftentimes our actions show such claims to be hollow and utilitarian. But this man lived with an ever-present cognizance of what exclusion looked, smelled, and felt like. I stopped second-guessing Ron and began to take reluctant small steps toward trusting him.

A first meaningful marker in our mentoring relationship occurred when Ron strongly encouraged me to submit an abstract to the first African American preconference of the Adult Education Research Conference to be held at Penn State. As is characteristic of him, he followed up. When he called several days before the abstract was due and asked to see my submission, I was too ashamed not to produce the work. Going to that conference, meeting black scholars and black professors, and seeming to belong was a turning point for me.

The definitive litmus test for our mentoring relationship was his response when I confided in him that I wanted to be a professor: he didn't laugh. He seemed to believe also, and most probably his belief in my ability to achieve this goal predated my acknowledgment and reclamation of this deferred dream.

We've come a long way since then, surviving every status change. Most mentoring relationships don't survive the natural maturation process, the occasional shift in role, and the inevitable blunders and missteps. I think that one very important reason for the durability of our relationship is that our association is multifaceted—a sociocultural context that encompasses struggle, reciprocity, learning, and scholarship.

Cross-Cultural Mentoring Relationships: Issues and Experiences

We now tell our shared story together to illuminate how social and cultural positionalities and power dynamics are inherent in a mentoring relationship. Juanita discusses the aspects of mentoring that she considers the most basic and crucial building blocks for a successful cross-cultural mentoring relationship: trust, understanding of the impact race has on the career of a minority academician, and the oppositional perspective of many marginalized faculty. Then Ron discusses the learning and power dimensions of mentoring, how the mentor benefits from this relationship, and the quandary faced by the mentor who must always be cognizant of how race frames the mentoring relationship while consistently looking past the issue of race.

Trust as the Essential Element of the Cross-Cultural Relationship. Establishing trust in a cross-cultural mentoring relationship is crucial to developing such a relationship, more so than in a same-race mentoring relationship (Bowman, Kite, Branscombe, and Williams, 2000; Brinson and Kottler, 1993; Thomas, 2001). On the surface, the concept of trust as it applies to mentoring appears simplistic: it needs to be reciprocal in nature and it's a matter between the mentor and protégé. However, in cross-cultural mentoring what should be a simple matter of negotiation between two persons becomes an arbitration between historical legacies, contemporary racial tensions, and societal protocols. A cross-cultural mentoring relationship is an affiliation between unequals who are conducting their relationship on a hostile American stage, with a societal script contrived to undermine the success of the partnership.

The historical legacy of relationships between black and white Americans is a one-sided scenario of mistrust. Black Americans have endured hundreds of years of suffering and abuse at the hands of white Americans who consistently espoused a mythical rhetoric of democracy and equality. Through hundreds of years of oppression, blacks remained loyal citizens, fighting in every war, working peacefully in often menial jobs, and waiting for the demise of Jim Crow so that they too could enjoy the American dream. Despite the myth of the violent angry black, it is white American citizens who have acted against blacks through legislated segregation, discriminatory customs, and mob violence (Franklin, 1956; Sitkoff, 1978). In essence, there is every reason for whites to be comfortable with (and yet to trust) blacks. There is very little reason for blacks to trust whites. It is against this backdrop of American history that trust must be built across the races before cross-cultural mentoring is to be attempted.

Initially we had to accept this circumstance as our own truth so that we would not be entrapped by such an inheritance. It was Juanita who had to trust Ron, and it was Juanita who was more at risk since she had less power and was therefore more vulnerable in the mentor-protégé ratio (Murrell and Tangri, 1999). The other component of the dynamic was that society supports the congruency of whites being in the more powerful position and encompasses set rules and expectations for a mixed-race relationship, in which deference and authority are essential components. Therefore a cross-cultural mentoring relationship can be negatively affected by unrecognized patterns of stereotypical behavior that is encoded in the American psyche, a paradigm that dictates "staying in one's place," refraining from being aggressive or threatening, and avoiding the perception of intimacy (Thomas, 2001). Trust was also a factor for Ron to consider. However, he was doubly protected from any possible risk by his status as a tenured full professor and his position as a white male.

Working through trust on the individual level is routinely discussed in the mentoring literature, but one must also recognize that the mentoring relationship is much broader than an association between two persons. Mentoring occurs on two dimensions: the internal aspect transpires between the mentor and the protégé; a second, external aspect takes place between the mentoring pair and their institution (O'Neill, Horton, and Crosby, 2000). Given that Ron and Juanita's working environment is a predominately white institution with a current record of court battles over affirmative action and racial quotas, the connection to the institution and its members is a weighty part of their mentoring union. In the tenuous atmosphere of their institution, Juanita has struggled with a hostile environment and contentious colleagues and watched in confusion, subdued anger, and resentment as Ron experienced that same setting with relative ease and a seeming degree of good cheer. The reality that the mentor and the protégé have differing experiences and reactions in their shared work environment is a source of unease and uncommon ground that can weaken the bonds of trust and set up an impasse of cyclical anger and guilt. Bowman, Kite, Branscombe, and Williams (2000) cite white guilt as a major impediment for a black-white mentoring team. However, the literature neglects to suggest why white guilt intrudes into a cross-cultural mentoring situation and also fails to propose any solution for the dilemma. White guilt, on the part of the mentor, could be a reaction to the awareness of unearned white privilege, or it might be a natural defensive reaction to black anger.

For an answer, it seems practical to refer to two frequently touted recommendations. One stresses the importance of ongoing and honest discussion about race and racism in cross-cultural mentoring situations. A second advises that the protégé be paired with a mentor with whom he or she shares a similar worldview. Indeed, the continuous foregrounding of candid conversation about race and the important stipulation of matching mentor and protégé on the basis of their life philosophies are plausible solutions for creating an environment where trust is likely to grow between like-minded individuals.

Racism as a Hidden Destructive Force in Cross-Cultural Mentoring. Race and racial group membership are defining markers in our world; consequently, these signs of membership and exclusion are powerful forces in the academy. However, race often remains invisible to the privileged white majority in academia, and racism in this setting is characteristically shrouded in rational discourse. When assessing the experiences of blacks in the academy, black faculty are routinely viewed as interlopers and rejected as rightful participants (Bowman, Kite, Branscombe, and Williams,

2000; Epps, 1989), and the circumstances of the academic lives of black faculty are marred with racist incidents, isolation, or benign indifference (Brinson and Kottler, 1993; Ragins, 1997). Thus racial group membership becomes a powerful force in the lives of minority faculty. To offset this uneasy state of black existence within the academy, Blake (2000) believes that it is essential for a cross-cultural mentoring team to spend considerable time and emotion acknowledging the burden of racism encountered by black academicians.

Certainly, an important factor that contributed to the early success of our own mentoring relationship was Ron's acceptance of Juanita's racist experiences as real and not the imagining of an oversensitive or paranoid black woman. He would listen (without offering any rationalizations) to her tales of being harassed by the campus police as she left her classroom, and of being rescued by a white student who vouched for her credibility. This psychosocial aspect of their relationship, wherein Ron counseled Juanita and demonstrated his acceptance of her narrative, helped to build a solid foundation (Kram, 1985; Smith, Smith, and Markham, 2000).

Fortuitously, a research agenda grew out of Ron and Juanita's conversations about race, and in turn it facilitated their personal discussion. When these issues arose, they were more easily mediated because the twosome had previously read and digested examples of the same. For example, mentoring articles address the varying cultural communication patterns, interpersonal styles, and cultural-racial-ethnic heritages that abound in cross-cultural mentoring relationships (Brinson and Kottler, 1993; Bowman, Kite, Branscombe, and Williams, 2000). Ron understood Juanita's culture-bound style of communicating through stories, which often took the scenic route in making a point. Juanita came to understand that Ron's brief answers, silences, and probing questions were not a sign of detachment but were part of his problem-solving technique and his composed approach to life.

Visibility, Risk, and Negotiation from the Margins. Academia is a hostile and unaccepting environment for minority faculty. Only 3 percent of all college and university faculty are black, and the majority of the meager 3 percent are concentrated in the junior ranks or else at historically black colleges and universities. Furthermore, black women are even more underrepresented, at less than 1 percent of college faculty (Bowman, Kite, Branscombe, and Williams, 2000; Menges and Exum, 1983). Although the number of minority students steadily increased over the past four decades, there has been no corresponding increase in the number of minority faculty. The literature notes that black women are more disadvantaged than their white female counterparts and their black male brethren because they experience the double impact of sexism and racism (Menges and Exum, 1983). In fact, black women in the academy have been characterized as being "isolated, underutilized, and often demoralized" (Carroll, 1973, p. 173).

The low percentage of black women faculty makes Juanita especially visible and susceptible to being solicited to serve on diversity committees, work on minority initiatives, and nurture minority students. Advising Juanita on which invitations to accept or refuse and how to weigh these decisions on the tenure scale has been part of Ron's vigilant stance as a mentor. Another jeopardy for Juanita is her race-based research agenda, which is perceived as provocative in conservative academic circles. Menges and Exum (1983) note that "unfortunately, but understandably, much of that provocation is experienced by senior academics as a threat. Junior professors seeking promotion and tenure are caught between obeying the maxim, 'Thou shalt not threaten senior colleagues,' and maintaining their integrity as scholars and teachers" (p. 135). For Juanita, part of this risk has been mitigated by the fact that she and Ron co-research many of these issues. In addition, an integral part of the acceptance of her work is due to his sponsorship of her. Brinson and Kottler (1993) regard this public endorsement of the protégé as an important part of the mentor's responsibilities.

Two other serious obstacles that have to be faced by minority protégés and white mentors are the paternalistic and political nature inherent in the mentoring process. The hierarchically prescribed mentor-protégé relationship resembles the paternalistic model of the authoritative superior and deferential subordinate that is a painful part of a racist American legacy. Many black faculty react negatively and almost unconsciously to this objectionable inequality (Brinson and Kottler, 1993; Margolis and Romero, 2001). Again, for Ron and Juanita an understanding of this societal pattern and a shared social justice worldview meant there was no place for paternalism. The trust in their relationship made the occasional hierarchical situation palatable, flexible, and at times unnoticeable.

From a sociopolitical perspective, a black woman like Juanita at a predominantly white institution "is incongruent with the racial distribution of power both in the institution and in the larger society within which the institution is embedded" (Murrell and Tangri, 1999, p. 215). Ron's position in the academy and his place as the superior in the mentoring pair fits with the hegemonic patterns of the university and does not create any great risk for him. However, his successful sponsorship of Juanita marks him simultaneously as a champion for the downtrodden and as a possible traitor who has broken with the ranks. Juanita's lifelong position of being on the margins of society has led her and many minority faculty to situate their lives in opposition to a society that devalues them (Johnson-Bailey, 1999). This resistance for survival's sake is frequently reflected in the research of scholars who are members of a disenfranchised group (Menges and Exum, 1983; Margolis and Romero, 2001). This oppositional lens of the faculty at the margin projects mentoring as an instrument of socialization wherein mentors "control the gates of social reproduction" (Margolis and Romero, 2001, p. 82). Mentors naturally seek to recreate their protégé in their own image, relying on a previously successful plan. But the attempted replication is an ill-fitting likeness for a minority protégé. To his credit, Ron always recognized and celebrated Juanita's difference and sought to find a way to optimize a fit between her talents and the academy. For example, he encouraged and advocated her culturally based work on narrative years before narrative was accepted as a valid methodological research approach. It has been Ron's ability to support his protégée and his ability to model a generous spirit of creativity and scholarship that has helped their mentoring relationship evolve through many phases and challenges.

Mentoring Relationships Are the Site of Struggle for Learning and Power. Most definitions frame the relationship between mentor and protégé as one of "intense caring," where a person with more experience works with a less experienced one to promote both personal and professional development (Hansman, 2001). However, this framing of the relationship in purely psychological terms, though partly true, ignores the central dynamic of any mentoring relationship, its hierarchical nature (Bowman, Kite, Branscombe, and Williams, 2000). This power relationship is further magnified in cross-cultural mentoring, where the people are in differing locations in societal hierarchies of race and gender. As Ragins (1997) explains, "Diversified mentoring relationships are composed of mentors and protégés who differ in group membership associated with power differences" (p. 482). As we have argued about all adult learning situations (Johnson-Bailey and Cervero, 1998), the power relations that structure our social lives cannot possibly be checked at the classroom door. Likewise, the learning dimensions of the cross-cultural mentoring relationship are enacted within the political and social hierarchies in which both people live. This has implications for both the instrumental learning and the psychosocial counseling that are part of an effective mentoring relationship (Thomas, 2001).

At the structural level, our mentoring relationship is hierarchical in terms of both race and gender, which is typical of how many black women are mentored (Blake, 2000). This type of relationship may occur since there are more white men in a position to mentor. Another explanation may be that white men can afford to be more generous with their time and power than others who are still negotiating access to high organizational levels. We recognize the interlocking nature of these societal hierarchies, and the aforementioned sexism of the culture, but our experience has been that gender plays a less significant role than does race as a site of struggle for learning and power. One way that race plays out is in the content of Juanita's need for mentoring, almost all of which has been about her experiences as a black person teaching white students. This mentoring takes the form of coaching about strategies for dealing with incidents that arise in her teaching as well as psychosocial counseling to process the negative ramifications of being verbally attacked by students.

Who Benefits? The Mentor as Learner. Virtually all of the literature about mentoring assumes a "teacher centered view of learning" (Margolis and Romero, 2001, p. 85). In fact, the very definitions of mentoring speak about "coaching and counseling" functions, which effectively define the learning as unidirectional. One problem with this understanding is that it is highly paternalistic in that the mentor is seen as above the fray. However, to be real and truly human, we need to understand that a relationship affects both people and that the mentor gains from the relationship: career enhancement, information exchange, recognition, and personal satisfaction (Smith, Smith, and Markham, 2000). Margolis and Romero (2001) point out it is rarely acknowledged that "mentoring is an agent of socialization and that part of the game of mirrors is that the mentor shines by reflection" (p. 84). Ragins (1997) has discussed three ways that the mentor benefits: in terms of diversity outcomes, intrinsic outcomes, and organizational outcomes. All mentors obtain intrinsic and organizational outcomes, but diversity outcomes are achieved only in a cross-cultural relationship. In particular, Brinson and Kottler (1993) argue that the mentor needs to develop a working knowledge of the protégé's culture and worldview, which in the long run benefits the mentor as well.

These diversity-related outcomes were particularly important in our relationship. As we discussed in the previous section, the major learning has related to the racial differences between us. Ron had to learn what it means to be a black faculty member at a university since his knowledge and experience was limited by his social condition of being white. Without this knowledge, he would engage in color-blind mentoring, which could prove to be detrimental to Juanita's development. For instance, the question of whether to pursue a research agenda based on issues of race plays out very differently for white and black faculty members. Black faculty members are often seen as having an agenda when they pursue this line of research, whereas white scholars are seen as progressive. Thus there is a "cultural taxation" (Padilla, 1994) for any ethnic or racial minority scholar; the mentor must understand this.

Seeing Race and Forgetting Race in a Mentoring Relationship. One key site of struggle for learning in a cross-cultural mentoring relationship "is the nature of [the] mentor's and the protégé's attitudes towards diversity" (Ragins, 1997, p. 506). In fact, studies (Bowman, Kite, Branscombe, and Williams, 2000; Thomas, 2001) have shown that mentors in cross-race relationships carry out career development and psychosocial functions when both members share similar understandings and strategies for dealing with racial differences in the relationship. However, when the mentor and protégé engage in "protective hesitation" (Thomas, 2001), where they refrain from raising touchy racial issues, then the relationship lacks psychosocial support. Bowman, Kite, Branscombe, and Williams (2000) say that an effective strategy when mentoring black Americans is to see the protégé as an individual and not as a category: "remember that they are Black Americans and forget that they are Black Americans" (p. 38). As we discussed in the section about the issue of trust, the protégé also needs to see the white mentor as an individual and not a category or representative of the larger white society.

We are congruent in our understanding of the role that race and racism play in American society (Johnson-Bailey and Cervero, 2000). We have argued in our research that although race is clearly a social construct, its effects are real in our daily lives. Our theoretical understanding of race is one factor that shows us how to both see race and forget race in our mentoring relationship. We recognize that although our racial differences are a necessary part of our daily interaction, we also can connect as people. We have learned that the first step in getting beyond the barriers and boundaries of race is not to pretend that they do not exist.

Implications for Mentoring and Learning

What implications can be drawn from our examination of cross-cultural mentoring? There are two major areas that encapsulate our discussion: the impact and significance of mentoring at the organizational and individual levels.

Most of the literature examines the individual dynamics of mentoring: issues concerning trust, risk, and matters of interpersonal style. Overall, the literature effectively analyzes the factors that influence the psychosocial and developmental components of mentoring. In sum, it is clear that mentoring benefits both parties. The protégé gains access to an experienced and expert guide; mentored faculty achieve more job success, report higher salaries, and have greater career mobility (Murrell and Tangri, 1999; Smith, Smith, and Markham, 2000). In exchange for his or her services, the mentor receives career enhancement, recognition, and personal satisfaction (Smith, Smith, and Markham, 2000). Indeed, both persons involved in the mentoring equation grow from the exposure to another culture and from the challenge of stepping outside of their comfort zone.

In terms of the rudimentary facets of mentoring, it is generally reported that the protégé is responsible for seeking a mentor and that faculty of color have difficulty obtaining a mentor (Bowman, Kite, Branscombe, and Williams, 2000; Margolis and Romero, 2001) because of the theory of homogeneity: people prefer to mentor those from their own ethnic group. Given the direct benefits imparted by mentoring, including cross-cultural mentoring, it is essential that new faculty be mentored. Therefore, we recommend a proactive stance from senior faculty who are willing to mentor their younger colleagues. We also suggest that new faculty be assertive in creating a mentoring consortium to fulfill their range of needs. Minority scholars can form self-mentoring groups (Margolis and Romero, 2001) or they can acquire other mentors to satisfy specific needs (Bowman, Kite, Branscombe, and Williams, 2000). For example, there might be a senior coworker who is good at understanding the organization's political landscape and another associate who is a dynamic teacher and classroom manager. Both colleagues would be indispensable in a collective of mentors.

Mentors in cross-cultural relationships must also understand that their job does not end with the individual protégé. As Thomas (2001) argues, the mentor must do more by actively supporting broad learning initiatives at the organization to help foster the upward mobility of people of color. For example, the mentor can promote workshops that address racial issues and support networking groups among racial minority faculty. This is a key strategy in changing the face of higher education so that it looks more like the society it serves.

Our mentoring experiences occurred at a Research One university, but the environment is nevertheless a workplace. We believe that our experiences and recommendations are applicable to any workplace, since grappling with power struggles, guarding one's turf, managing diversity, making on-the-job adjustments, learning, changing, and growing are not exclusive to the university setting.

References

Blake, S. "At the Crossroads of Race and Gender: Lessons from the Mentoring Experiences of Professional Black Women." In A. J. Murrell, F. J. Crosby, and R. J. Ely (eds.), *Mentoring Dilemmas: Developmental Relationships Within Multicultural Organizations.* Mahwah, N.J.: Erlbaum, 2000.

Bowman, S. R., Kite, M. E., Branscombe, N. R., and Williams, S. "Developmental Relationships of Black Americans in the Academy." In A. J. Murrell, F. J. Crosby, and R. J. Ely (eds.), *Mentoring Dilemmas: Developmental Relationships Within Multicultural Organizations.* Mahwah, N.J.: Erlbaum, 2000.

Brinson, J., and Kottler, J. "Cross-Cultural Mentoring in Counselor Education: A Strategy for Retaining Minority Faculty." *Counselor Education and Supervision,* 1993, *32* (4), 241–254.

Carroll, C. M. "Three's a Crowd: The Dilemma of the Black Woman in Higher Education." In A. S. Rossi and A. Calderwood (eds.), *Academic Women on the Move.* New York: Russell Sage Foundation, 1973.

Epps, E. "Academic Culture and the Minority Professor." *Academe,* 1989, *36* (5), 23–26.

Franklin, J. H. *From Slavery to Freedom: A History of American Negroes.* New York: Knopf, 1956.

Hansman, C. C. "Who Plans? Who Participates? Critically Examining Mentoring Programs." In R. O. Smith, J. M. Dirkx, P. L. Eddy, P. L. Farrell, and M. Polzin (eds.), *Proceedings of the 42nd Annual Adult Education Research Conference.* East Lansing: Michigan State University, 2001.

Johnson-Bailey, J. "The Ties That Bind and the Shackles That Separate: Race, Gender, Class, and Color in a Research Process." *Qualitative Studies in Education,* 1999, *12* (6), 659–670.

Johnson-Bailey, J., and Cervero, R. M. "Power Dynamics in Teaching and Learning Practices: An Examination of Two Adult Education Classrooms." *International Journal of Lifelong Education,* 1998, *17* (6), 389–399.

Johnson-Bailey, J., and Cervero, R. M. "The Invisible Politics of Race in Adult Education." In A. L. Wilson and E. R. Hayes (eds.), *Handbook of Adult and Continuing Education: New Edition.* San Francisco: Jossey Bass, 2000.

Kram, K. E. *Mentoring at Work.* Glenview, Ill.: Scott, Foresman, 1985.

Margolis, E., and Romero, M. "In the Image and Likeness: How Mentoring Functions in the Hidden Curriculum." In E. Margolis (ed.), *The Hidden Curriculum in Higher Education.* New York: Routledge, 2001.

McIntosh, P. "White Privilege and Male Privilege: A Personal Accounting of Coming to See Correspondences Through Work in Women's Studies." In M. L. Anderson and P. H. Collins (eds.), *Race, Class, and Gender.* Belmont, Calif.: Wadsworth, 1995.

Menges, R., and Exum, W. H. "Barriers to the Progress of Women and Minority Faculty." *Journal of Higher Education,* 1983, *54* (2), 123–144.

Murrell, A. J., and Tangri, S. S. "Mentoring at the Margin." In A. J. Murrell, F. J. Crosby, and R. J. Ely (eds.), *Mentoring Dilemmas: Developmental Relationships Within Multicultural Organizations.* Mahwah, N.J.: Erlbaum, 1999.

O'Neill, R. N., Horton, S., and Crosby, F. J. "Gender Issues in Developmental Relationships." In A. J. Murrell, F. J. Crosby, and R. J. Ely (eds.), *Mentoring Dilemmas: Developmental Relationships Within Multicultural Organizations.* Mahwah, N.J.: Erlbaum, 2000.

Padilla, A. M. "Ethnic Minority Scholars, Research, and Mentoring." *Educational Researcher,* 1994, *23* (4), 24–27.

Ragins, B. R. "Diversified Mentoring Relationships in Organizations: A Power Perspective." *Academy of Management Review,* 1997, *22,* 482–521.

Sitkoff, H. *A New Deal for Blacks—The Emergence of Civil Rights as a National Issue: The Depression Decade.* New York: Oxford University Press, 1978.

Smith, J. W., Smith, W. J., and Markham, S. E. "Diversity Issues in Mentoring Academic Faculty." *Journal of Career Development,* 2000, *26* (4), 251–262.

Thomas, D. A. "The Truth About Mentoring Minorities: Race Matters." *Harvard Business Review,* Apr. 2001, pp. 99–107.

JUANITA JOHNSON-BAILEY is an associate professor of adult education and women's studies at the University of Georgia, Athens.

RONALD M. CERVERO is a professor and department head of adult education at the University of Georgia, Athens.

3

In the field of adult education, the context of immigration as it influences the learning experiences of foreign-born learners has received scant attention. This chapter examines the influence of early formal and informal socialization on the learning behavior of immigrants and second language learners in U.S. adult education.

Socialization and Immigrant Students' Learning in Adult Education Programs

Ming-Yeh Lee, Vanessa Sheared

In the field of adult education, the effects of race, class, gender, and sexual orientation on student learning have been widely explored (Hayes and Flannery, 2000; Guy, 1999; Johnson-Bailey and Cervero, 1996; Sheared, 1994; Tisdell, 1993). However, literature on cultural and linguistic differences and learning among immigrant adult students is rare (Alfred, 2000; Hvitfeldt, 1986), and literature that addresses the impact of formal and informal socialization on immigrants and second language learners is even more limited.

The intent of this chapter is to give the practitioner concrete suggestions to effectively meet the needs of immigrant adult learners. To this end, we present a historic overview of immigrants in the United States, with specific emphasis on the educational programs offered in this country as a direct response to the various waves of immigrants, and we examine how culture and socialization affect learning.

To give you some context about our claim of the importance of examining this topic, we open with a brief story about one of us. Although the experiences of the first author are explored here,[1] we believe that, rather than focus as well on the experiences of the second author, we should "give voice" to the individual who has been most affected by informal and formal socialization of a foreign-born, linguistically diverse learner. For us, it is clear that even though Vanessa's contribution to this article was important, it is Ming-Yeh's experiences in this area we most need to articulate.

NEW DIRECTIONS FOR ADULT AND CONTINUING EDUCATION, no. 96, Winter 2002 © Wiley Periodicals, Inc.

Insights from an Insider

Because English is not my first language, I (Ming-Yeh) asked my colleague to work with me on this project as a way to articulate for ourselves, as well as others, the significance of providing a voice to an area of great concern to me. This area became of particular interest to me during my first semester of doctoral studies. As a student attempting to grapple with the nuances and subtleties of the English language as well as the cultural norms of American students, I became increasingly aware of how my cultural text was constantly being challenged by others. A student of American English as a first language pressed me to respond to a question on the worksheet in a discussion group. Before I had a chance to respond, she added, in a rushing tone, "Why do you hardly say anything in the class?" A dead silence came over the group. Suddenly, without my saying anything, the discussion moved on. The episode was over for them in about two minutes, but for me there was a lingering effect. I still recall the strong sense of isolation I felt.

I learned during those minutes that although I thought I had successfully learned how to fit in, it was clear that I had not learned the formal language skills needed to confront such a situation. To this day, even though now I have my doctoral degree, I still feel this sense of isolation.

Like many taken-for-granted behaviors and thoughts, this silent learning style was developed during my childhood. According to Goodenough (1971), one learns the formal and informal socialization skills needed to survive in any given learning situation. He goes on to say, "the standards for deciding what is, standards for deciding what can be, standards for deciding how one feels about it, standards for deciding what to do about it and standards for deciding how to go about doing it" (p. 19) are grounded in one's cultural norms. Therefore, when there is a cultural gap between previous and current learning settings, those learners who have to cross cultural borders are usually judged differently by others.

This becomes even more significant when we look at how we work with individuals whose first language is not English. Those teaching individuals whose primary language is not English, and whose socialization patterns have been developed in another country, must pay attention to how we can use formal and informal socialization to help them perform effectively as students in our classrooms.

Historical Overview of Immigrant Adult Students in U.S. Education

America is considered a country of immigrants. Indeed, approximately sixty million immigrants have come to the United States since its founding (Martin and Midgley, 1994). Before World War II, the majority of immigrants came voluntarily and were initially of European descent, from the

British Isles and Northern European countries and ultimately Eastern and Southern Europe (Orem, 1991).

However, the gate of this newly "discovered" continent has never been a place easily accessible to people of color, or those whose language was not English. The first laws concerning immigration in the United States were passed in 1790, to restrict naturalization rights to "free white persons" only. In the late nineteenth century and early twentieth century, eight acts were passed to forbid Chinese and Japanese immigrants from entering or being naturalized as U.S. citizens (Amott and Matthaei, 1996).

Wars, international tension, and various sociopolitical factors have had an impact on how immigration is addressed in the United States. One of the most significant movements occurred during the late nineteenth and early twentieth centuries, during which programs were developed to help immigrants become acculturated. This "Americanization" movement was aimed at helping immigrants acclimate and learn the language, cultural norms, and values of the United States. As Orem (1991) notes, the Americanization movement "primarily stemmed from the public's growing concerns about the 'alien' ideas, values, and languages brought in by the new waves of Eastern and Southern European immigrants" (p. 491). Schools offered adult ESL (English as a second language) courses as part of the Americanization curriculum, and to help indoctrinate the new immigrants into Anglo-Saxon–based "American" ways to ensure their acculturation (Stubblefield and Keane, 1994). Passage of immigration laws after World War II led to elimination of restrictions on many immigrants, particularly those of Asian ancestry. In fact, during the 1980s there was an influx of immigrants from Mexico, the Philippines, China, Korea, and Vietnam (Martin and Midgley, 1994).

This new wave of immigrants reflects a polarized demographic pattern between the most educated and wealthiest and the least educated and poorest. The more wealth and education one has, the smoother the transition into the U.S. cultural milieu. On the other hand, the less educated and poorer the immigrant, the more likely it is that government intervention will be needed. However, whether one is poor or wealthy, educated or not, programs aimed at this population need to focus on helping immigrants make a smooth transition from their home to the host country. This requires a strong emphasis on survival issues, including basic life skills, vocational training (Steward, 1993), and other adult education programs. This requires that we have a clear understanding of how cultural values influence learning among foreign-born students, who received their early socialization in non-Western cultures.

Cultural Models of Learning

Cultural models describe how cultural values and beliefs strongly affect, but do not directly determine, one's thoughts, attitudes, and behaviors within the socialization process. A cultural model generally refers to the system of cultural knowledge, values, beliefs, and behavior norms acquired by people belonging to a particular cultural group. According to Quinn and Holland (1987), this term refers to the action taking and meaning making of the individual within a particular group setting. Cultural models have psychological power to motivate and affect the behavior of the individual within the group. Again, it is important to stress the fact that a cultural model can only affect, but never completely determine, a person's behavior within the group (D'Andrade, 1992). For instance, vague cultural messages can be interpreted incorrectly if the message is given outside of a familiar sociocultural context (D'Andrade and Strauss, 1992). In other words, one's cultural understanding is acquired through socialization.

Using cultural models is a relatively new concept in the field of adult education. For instance, Alfred (2000) employed the concept to help her gain insights as to how British Caribbean immigrant women perceive the way in which their earliest socialization in school was instrumental in shaping their learning preferences and identities as adult learners in Western cultures. Having been socialized in a British schooling culture that fostered competition and objective knowing, the women in her study preferred learning through written format and in isolation.

Hvitfeldt (1986) investigated the impact of cultural factors on newly immigrated Hmong adults' learning experience. Similarly, Hvitfeldt suggests that being socialized in a preindustrial and preliterate society profoundly affects how Hmong adults interact among themselves and with their instructors in the classroom. Their behaviors significantly reflect their distinctive ways of perceiving reality, processing information, and relating to others.

When students are placed in a context where another culture prevails, students may either resist initially or need more time for adjustment. The significance of the cultural model to the field of adult education, then, is that it can give us better understanding of how formal and informal socialization affect one's learning preference, interaction, and expectations in an adult classroom setting. We must also keep in mind that these learning preferences may be quite in contrast to the expectations of learners in the adult education classroom, resulting in a gap between the learner's native culture and the school culture.

Cultural Discontinuity and Learning

Cultural discontinuity suggests that a cultural gap or difference exists between learners' native culture and their current school culture. This often causes a student to feel marginalized, confused, and isolated. The feeling of marginality has been found to affect the development of student self-concept and academic performance and has been used to explain low academic performance and a high dropout rate among minority and immigrant students (for example, Erickson, 1987; McDermott, 1987).

Cummins (1986) and Delgado-Gaitan and Trueba (1991) found that the cultural difference or incongruence alone does not necessary cause a harmful impact on students. The damage (such as lowered performance) is caused by how teachers and instructors view and deal with the cultural gap. For instance, Amstutz (1999) and Guy (1999) have argued that the dominant culture has the power to define the behavioral norms, expectations, and values of the school culture; therefore, those with cultural differences are usually interpreted as unfit, inferior, or "less than." It is not a surprise, then, to find minority and immigrant students who feel isolated and incompetent in certain school contexts.

In summary, cultural differences exist between immigrant students' culture and the Euro-American culture in schools and society. The degree of cultural difference between teachers and student and the student reaction to the cultural difference contributes to how students perceive their culture, learning experience, and themselves. According to Ogbu (1987), learners may differ in their learning experience as a result of their immigration experience in the United States. Therefore, seeing the context of immigration for various immigrant groups is important in understanding the motivational patterns and the learning behaviors of group members.

Cultural Ecology and Learning

Cultural ecology (Ogbu, 1978, 1987) offers a contextual explanation for the variance in academic performance among minority and immigrant groups. The public tends to lump all immigrants into one group, but Ogbu categorizes minority and immigrant populations as being either "voluntary" or "involuntary." A person is voluntary if she or he enters the United States by choice, and involuntary if brought by force. For instance, African Americans and Mexican Americans are labeled involuntary because of forced relocation through slavery, colonization, and conquest.

The major difference between voluntary and involuntary status is in one's "folk story." The story of how one comes to and survives in the United States is an important factor in determining the opportunities one has here. Voluntary members tend to assimilate if their skin color, language, and hair are similar to those of people in the new country. They believe that if they work hard, then they will obtain economic and social benefits within their society. Once they overcome their cultural and language differences, they assimilate quickly to the cultural norms. In contrast, involuntary groups have learned through history and experience with Euro-Americans that their academic efforts may not be equally rewarded. Interestingly, in spite of seeking to learn the new language, the involuntary group comes to understand that their skin color (and sometimes even their hair texture) can prevent them from assimilating. For this reason, they often learn to resist and develop ways of coping for survival and identity, exclusive of assimilation.

Implications for the Adult Education Practitioner

Students' formal or informal socialization patterns directly affect their learning preference, role expectation, interaction pattern, and self-perception as learner. Having experienced the similar phenomenon of cultural difference, some learners achieve academic success while others do not (Cummins, 1986). Fordham and Ogbu (1986), and Ogbu (1978, 1987) argue that foreign-born learners' socioeconomic status, immigrant status, and how they operate within a school are highly correlated with academic performance and success. If this is so, then we in adult education need to understand the impact that formal and informal socialization have on the immigrant adult learner's cognitive and affective learning processes. With that in mind, we have identified five key steps that a teacher working with adult learners should take.

Design Inclusive Curriculum. The curriculum one designs for work with immigrant populations must acknowledge ethnicity, various cultural perspectives, and language. To affirm the foreign-born adult learner's experience and cultural heritage, citing historical events and antecedents is particularly useful. In one ESL program, the teacher relied upon students' cultural knowledge to help them learn connections to the historical events being discussed in class. The teacher used several books representing contrasting perspectives to challenge student thinking and help them understand that multiple answers could be given. The students then began to understand how Euro-centered discourse has presented distorted stories about themselves as well as others.

The curriculum materials must portray the lived experiences of, and give voice to, the immigrant learner (Sheared, 1994). Teachers should ask how the readings they've selected reflect the students' lived experiences. Are the images of the students reflected in the materials, or are they stereotypical? Instructors must finally ask whose interests the curriculum serves.

Examine Cultural Assumptions. The influence of socialization is forceful and enduring; what's more, both formal and informal experiences shape the adult educator's need to examine his or her own cultural assumptions in relation to teaching practice. For this reason, the adult educator must begin viewing the school culture as a site of contestation, a place where immigrant adult learners come not only to learn a new language or receive technical training but also to begin understanding and further challenging how schooling affects them.

For instance, some students of Asian ancestry, or Asian students who have recently immigrated to the United States, may have difficulty participating in open discussion. To participate in such a discussion or free response is not a common activity among many of these students. In these learners' native cultural setting, learning activities are often didactic; dialogue or discussion is a rarity. In that setting, the student becomes accustomed to remaining silent, listening, taking notes, and memorizing information.

Therefore the student's silence or lack of participation in discussion should not be interpreted as a lack of interest, preparation, or even ability to learn. Moreover, silence can be a sign of respect.

Thus the meaning of silence needs to be interpreted in the foreign-born learner's cultural context. For instance, silence manifested by a Chinese student may be explained by the expression, "the half bottle of water rattling and the whole bottle silenced." This saying reflects the typical Chinese attitude of affirming humility by refusing to brag about one's knowledge. So rather than expect such students to express themselves orally, which means showing off, the teacher might use alternative strategies to solicit participation. The teacher might allow the students more time so they can contemplate the best answer and avoid losing face as well.

Alfred's research (2002) offers yet another example of how silence is encouraged in some Caribbean societies and classrooms, where students generally express themselves mainly through written rather than oral discourse, as such dialogue and critique is often viewed as inappropriate public confrontation and poses a threat to the power and authority of the teacher. What's more, for women it can be viewed as "unladylike" to critique and challenge the knowledge of authority, in formal or informal settings (Alfred, 2002). Consequently, adult educators should not impose their own views about student classroom behavior out of context.

Promote Community Development and Involvement. "Marginalization and isolation" (Sheared, 1994) characterize many adult students' initial learning experiences. This is especially true for immigrants who begin attending classes within one to two years of arrival in the host country (Trueba and Bartolome, 2000). Creating a learning environment that allows students to see themselves engaged in a collective body can decrease the sense of competition that often characterizes the learning environment. Giving voice often leads to students formulating a sense of community because they begin to recognize and understand what connects them to, and separates them from, each other. For immigrant adult learners, especially if they have the same language or dialect, there is a likelihood that some form of community may be created within the class. This sense of community affords them a safe environment to test ways to behave with one another. Community development helps immigrant adult learners create beneficial social networks and resource circles. By designing participatory activity (discussions, panels, picture stories), the instructor can create an opportunity for students to bring their social personal history into the classroom environment.

Through community engagement, a teacher can help foreign-born adult learners extend their boundaries beyond the classroom. The participants in a community-based family literacy program we worked with were actively involved in various stages of program planning, including identifying learning topics and scheduling activities. We believed it was important to understand that students knew what they wanted, and that the topics chosen had to be of significance to them in their daily lives. The participants in this program identified violence resolution, communication with kids and schools, assisting kids with homework, and valuing cultural heritage as areas of concern for them in their community. We covered these topics through discussion, role play, brainstorming, and photo storytelling. By connecting with these learners' lived experiences and English as a second language literacy needs, the program became a site for active learning and critical reflection.

To create community, an instructor might ask the students to examine certain questions: "What strengths does my first language provide? "When or where should I use my first and second languages?" "What are the strengths and weaknesses of using English or my first language in my home?" By discussing these questions in class, the learner is likely to develop a critical perspective concerning the use of his or her first or second language. Rather than being a passive learner of the English language, one becomes an active author of the word and gains power over one's interaction with others whose first language is English.

Conclusion

Formal and informal socialization have a significant effect on immigrant adult learners in terms of how they see themselves as learners and participants in society and school. Given the increasing number of new immigrants to this country, adult educators must begin to examine how cultural models, the level of cultural discontinuity, and cultural ecology influence student interaction within the classroom. We are beginning to address and respond to the cultural differences among students' original culture, the teacher's understanding of his or her own cultural norms, and how the two affect learning within a formal learning setting. In addition, the teacher must make the class a community and involve the learners in thinking about what they want and need to learn. This may be difficult in the beginning, but in so doing the teacher can begin to capitalize on both formal and informal learning arrangements, which affect student learning and academic achievement. The concepts of cultural model, cultural discontinuity, and cultural ecology can shed some light on how an adult educator might begin to reconceptualize and structure the classroom.

Note

1. Two women, one of Asian ancestry born in Taiwan and the other of African ancestry born in America, wrote the chapter. We agreed to collaborate on this chapter, but we believe it is important to note that the lived experience of an immigrant learner as seen through the eyes of the immigrant are important. Therefore, we have used a learning experience from Ming-Yeh to accentuate the importance of this story.

References

Alfred, M. "The Politics of Knowledge and Theory Construction in Adult Education: A Critical Analysis from an Africentric Feminist Perspective." Forty-First Annual Adult Education Research Conference Proceedings, University of British Columbia, June 2000.

Alfred, M. "Epistemology and Social Context: Anglophone Caribbean Women and Their Learning and Development Across Cultural Borders." Unpublished manuscript, University of Wisconsin-Milwaukee, 2002.

Amott, T., and Matthaei, J. Race, Gender, and Work: A Multicultural Economic History of Women in the United States. Boston: South End Press, 1996.

Amstutz, D. "Adult Learning: Moving Toward More Inclusive Theories and Practices." In T. C. Guy (ed.), Providing Culturally Relevant Adult Education: A Challenge for the Twenty-First Century. New Directions for Adult and Continuing Education, no. 82. San Francisco: Jossey-Bass, 1999.

Cummins, J. "Empowering Minority Students: A Framework for Intervention." Harvard Educational Review, 1986, 56 (1), 18–36.

D'Andrade, R. G. "Schemas and Motivation." In R. G. D'Andrade and C. Strauss (eds.), Human Motives and Cultural Models. Cambridge: Cambridge University Press, 1992.

D'Andrade, R. G., and Strauss, C. (eds.). Human Motives and Cultural Models. Cambridge: Cambridge University Press, 1992.

Delgado-Gaitan, C., and Trueba, H. Crossing Cultural Borders: Education for Immigrant Families in America. London: Falmer, 1991.

Erickson, F. "Transformation and School Success." Anthropology and Education Quarterly, 1987, 18 (6), 335–355.

Fordham, S., and Ogbu, J. "Black Students' School Success: Coping with the Burden of Acting White." Urban Review, 1986, 18 (3), 176–206.

Goodenough, W. H. "Culture, Language, and Society." Addison-Wesley Module in Anthropology, 1971, 7, 1–48.

Guy, T. C. "Culture as Context for Adult Education: The Need for Culturally Relevant Adult Education." In T. C. Guy (ed.), Providing Culturally Relevant Adult Education: A Challenge for the Twenty-First Century. New Directions for Adult Continuing Education, no. 82. San Francisco: Jossey-Bass, 1999.

Hayes, E., and Flannery, D. (with Brooks, W. K., Tisdell, E. J., and Hugo, J.). Women as Learners. San Francisco: Jossey-Bass, 2000.

Hvitfeldt, C. "Traditional Culture, Perceptual Style, and Learning: The Classroom Behavior of Hmong Adults." Adult Education Quarterly, 1986, 36 (2), 65–77.

Johnson-Bailey, J., and Cervero, R. "An Analysis of the Educational Narratives of Reentry Black Women." Adult Education Quarterly, 1996, 46 (4), 142–158.

Martin, P., and Midgley, E. "Immigration to the United States: Journey to an Uncertain Destination." Population Bulletin, 1994, 49 (2), 2–46.

McDermott, R. P. "The Explanation of Minority School Failure, Again." Anthropology and Education Quarterly, 1987, 18 (4), 361–364.

Ogbu, J. U. Minority Education and Caste: The American System in Cross-Cultural Perspective. New York: Academic Press, 1978.

Ogbu, J. U. "Variability in Minority School Performance: A Problem in Search of an Explanation." Anthropology and Education Quarterly, 1987, 18 (6), 312–334.

Orem, R. "English as a Second Language." In P. M. Cunningham and S. B. Merriam (eds.), Handbook of Adult and Continuing Education. San Francisco: Jossey-Bass, 1991.

Quinn, N., and Holland, D. "Culture and Cognition." In D. Holland and N. Quinn (eds.), Cultural Models in Language and Thought. New York: Cambridge University Press, 1987.

Quinn, N., and Holland, D. "Culture and Cognition." In D. Holland and N. Quinn (eds.), *Cultural Models in Language and Thought*. New York: Cambridge University Press, 1987.

Sheared, V. "Giving Voice: An Inclusive Model of Instruction—A Womanist Perspective." In E. Hayes and S.A.J. Colin III (eds.), *Confronting Racism and Sexism in Adult Education*. New Directions for Continuing Education, no 61. San Francisco: Jossey-Bass, 1994.

Steward, D. W. *Immigration and Education: the Crisis and the Opportunities*. New York: Lexington, 1993.

Stubblefield, H. W., and Keane, P. *Adult Education in the American Experience: From the Colonial Period to the Present*. San Francisco: Jossey-Bass, 1994.

Tisdell, E. "Interlocking Systems of Power, Privilege, and Oppression in Adult Higher Education Classes." *Adult Education Quarterly*, 1993, 43 (4), 203–226.

Trueba, T., and Bartolome, L. (eds.). *Immigrant Voices: In Search of Educational Equity*. Lanham, Md.: Rowman and Littlefield, 2000.

U.S. Census Bureau. "2000 Population Estimate." U.S. Census Bureau, Population Division, 2000. (http://eire.census.gove/popest/estimates.php)

MING-YEH LEE *is an assistant professor in the Center for Adult Education, Department of Administration and Interdisciplinary Studies, at San Francisco State University.*

VANESSA SHEARED *is a professor in adult education and an associate dean for academic affairs at San Francisco State University.*

4

In this chapter, the author uses her own experiences as an adult learner in cyberspace to explore the social and cultural contexts of gender and national origin in adult learning.

The Sociocultural Implications of Learning and Teaching in Cyberspace

Simone Conceição

Over a decade ago, I voluntarily immigrated to the United States from Brazil for purposes of educational growth and emancipation. I was born and raised in a metropolitan area of southern Brazil that I would describe as progressive regarding its commitment to social reform on behalf of the poor. However, leadership opportunities for women were minimal, reflecting the social and cultural beliefs of traditional male-dominated Brazilian society, where men hold leadership positions in political, administrative, and business settings and women perform the traditional role of caretaker in the home and workplace (Hayes, 2001). Feeling powerless to move on professionally, I decided to obtain education in a new context.

Even though immigrating to the United States freed me somewhat from traditional female roles, it challenged my assumptions about my learning. I came from a culture where group cooperation was emphasized, time was relative, thinking was holistic, affective expression was evident, extended family was the norm, the worldviews of other cultures were generally accepted, and interactions were socially oriented. In Brazilian culture, I displayed a field-dependent cognitive learning style, which is relational, holistic, and highly affective. A cognitive style comprises perception and personality and affects interpersonal behavior and the way a person processes information. A field-dependent cognitive style is characterized by a personality that presents characteristics of being socially dependent, eager to make a good impression, conforming, and sensitive to social surroundings. Conversely, field-independent and analytic thinking with limited affective thinking are characteristics of the Euro-American cognitive learning style (Sanchez and Gunawardena, 1998).

NEW DIRECTIONS FOR ADULT AND CONTINUING EDUCATION, no. 96, Winter 2002   © Wiley Periodicals, Inc.

Moving to the United States and joining its higher education system required that I adapt and expand my learning style to accommodate the independent cognitive learning style of my new environment. Cyberspace education was central to these changes in my learning. During my years of graduate study in adult education, I discovered that learning how to use a computer was instinctive to me; later, online education became a way to communicate and interact with others in a socially independent environment since its social activities are independent of time.

Contrary to the educational system in the United States, my previous experiences in the sociocultural context of Brazilian education entailed progressing through college with the same group of classmates, the *turma* (cohort) approach, from entrance to graduation. The American system of education posed a different social infrastructure. This change in infrastructure required a shift in my learning approach; for instance, I had to be self-regulated. Technology allowed me to adapt to the new learning style by becoming a more independent and task-oriented person. In the process, I realized that using computers as a tool for learning and communicating, and cyberspace as the context of learning, was transformative and emancipatory.

In this chapter, I use my own experiences as an adult learner in cyberspace and the adult education literature to explore the social and cultural contexts of gender and national origin and their implications for learning within an online community. I draw from the individual and the contextual approach to learning as the perspectives to guide reflection on my experiences within the context of adult education. I conclude the chapter by offering practical implications of learning and teaching in cyberspace.

Defining Cyberspace

In this chapter, *cyberspace* refers to the online environment that is accessible to learners and instructors who are separated by time and physical distance. Cyberspace learning involves using personal computers (clients) linked to a central host computer (server) by a local network, telephone line, or data network. The instructor and learners use their client computers and modems to connect to the server. The server runs a conferencing software program such as WebBoard or First Class or a course management software tool such as Blackboard Course Info, WebCT, or Learning Space. Learners have twenty-four-hour access to the server and can connect to it to receive messages from or post messages to other participants. Online learning assumes participation in instruction that is entirely online, without face-to-face interaction.

Perspectives of Learning

According to Caffarella and Merriam (2000), learning in adulthood is usually studied from two perspectives. One focuses on the learner as individual, while the other centers on the contextual approach to learning. The first perspective looks at the learner and responds to individual learning styles to help adults learn efficiently. The contextual perspective focuses on two dimensions, the *interactive* and *structural*. The interactive dimension recognizes learning as a product of the individual interacting with the context of learning, while the structural dimension acknowledges the social and cultural aspects that influence learning, such as race, class, gender, ethnicity, and power and oppression (Caffarella and Merriam, 2000).

Since the adult education literature that is related to these perspectives make little reference to learners' experiences in cyberspace, adult educators are beginning to raise questions as they design and deliver such instruction (Caffarella and Merriam, 2000; Merriam and Caffarella, 1999; Hansman, 2001). My own experiences as a learner in cyberspace, guided by the individual and contextual approaches to learning and the current adult education literature, may provide some insight to this phenomenon of learning in an online environment.

My Perspective as a Cyberlearner

My perspective as an individual learner in cyberspace is based on three major concepts: (1) participation and motivation are necessary to function in an environment that lacks physical presence, (2) self-direction is necessary for successful learning without face-to-face interaction, and (3) transformational learning allows personal and social construction of knowledge because of the opportunity to interact with others (Caffarella and Merriam, 2000; Garrison, 1997; Clark, 1993).

Participation and Motivation. Participation in cyberspace is typically through written communication. Contributions to class activity are reading and writing assignments. For instance, comments are documented, succinct, and pithy thanks to the logical structure of the language (Conceição-Runlee and Reilly, 1999).

Motivation is defined by Garrison (1997) as the "perceived value and anticipated success of learning goals at the time learning is initiated and mediated between context (control) and cognition (responsibility) during the learning process" (p. 26). Thus, motivation plays an important function in initiating and maintaining effort toward learning in cyberspace. As someone coming from an affective and relational culture, I depended on extrinsic motivation, fueled by outside rewards. In cyberspace, I had to rely on intrinsic motivation to overcome the fact that the emotional dimension of a message (humor, disagreement, and the like) could be lost or misinterpreted without verbal and visual cues, body language, or intonation (Conceição-Runlee and Reilly, 1999).

Self-Directed Learning. I recognize self-directed learning as a central concept in cyberspace. I first believed that being a learner in cyberspace involved loneliness and detachment because of the individualized nature of working in front of a computer. However, with time, my experience as an online learner revealed that there is no time to feel lonely or detached unless I lacked motivation to participate in the interaction or self-direction to complete an assignment.

According to Garrison (1997), self-directed learning is defined as "an approach where learners are motivated to assume personal responsibility and collaborative control of the cognitive (self-monitoring) and contextual (self-management) processes in constructing and confirming meaningful and worthwhile outcomes" (p. 18). Depending on the structure of the course management tool, the navigational design of the course, and the assignments developed by the instructor, I was able to make decisions (self-monitoring) about what to learn, how to learn it, and when to learn it. This meant I was responsible for the internal cognitive and motivational aspects of my own learning. I was free to navigate through the online course environment with autonomy. In other words, the online learning activity emphasized cognitive freedom and promoted learning how to learn (Garrison, 1997).

In addition to self-monitoring, self-directed learning entails self-management of learning resources and support. Garrison (1997) states that self-management "involves shaping the contextual conditions in the performance of goal-directed actions" (p. 23). In my experience as a learner, I was able to manage control of activities in using learning materials within the online environment. Furthermore, self-management increased my control over my learning, which in turn meant increased responsibility. From my own observation as a learner, control over and responsibility for my learning were essential to the success of my performance in cyberspace. These skills helped me become task-oriented once I understood the design (organization and structure) of the text-based environment.

Transformational Learning. The third concept related to the individual learner is transformational learning. I considered my experience as a learner in cyberspace a transformational one. Before my cyberspace experience, the meaning of learning was for me based on a traditional classroom setting with participants of the teaching and learning process present in the same room. Learning online involved adapting to a new way of learning and making meaning of the new experience through critical self-reflection and social interaction.

Mezirow (1998) writes that critical self-reflection of assumptions means "a premise upon which the learner has defined a problem" (p. 186). In my case, I had previously assumed that for learning to occur it was supposed to take place in an environment where learners and instructor would see each other. Cyberspace learning, then, was an issue for me initially since learners and instructors were physically absent.

My first online class focused on the adult independent learner. The course involved general course interactions, online discussion with group members, a group project, and a reflective paper. My classmates and I were constantly reflecting on the meaning of online learning, the advantages and limitations of cyberspace, and the experiences we were gaining or missing because of the lack of physical presence. The social interactions with my classmates in cyberspace were part of our reflective conversation.

Clark (1993) believes that "transformation is about change, so transformational learning must be related to learning that produces change" (p. 47). For me, the online learning process involved a perspective transformation, a response to an imposed disorienting dilemma (Mezirow, 1990) evoked by the new mode of learning. Mezirow defines disorienting dilemma as a life crisis or major life event transition. Learning online became a trigger event in my life, involving sitting in front of my computer interacting with people unseen, writing in a language somewhat unnatural to me, and interpreting message and meaning without the benefit of facial expressions or vocal tone. I then engaged in the process of critical self-reflection and evaluation of assumptions about my own learning style. Through this process, I realized that learning online involved a change in beliefs and values about instruction, which resulted in a perspective transformation in my view of what teaching and learning meant in the new environment. Since part of my self-reflection involved engaging in "reflective discourse" with my classmates, I was living the new perspective just by being an online learner (Baumgartner, 2001).

Functioning in cyberspace required that I understand and interpret the online environment in order to perform the appropriate learning task through instrumental learning, which Mezirow (1990) defines as "the process of learning to control and manipulate the environment or other people" (p. 8). At the same time, I needed to develop communicative learning skills, or the ability to understand the values; ideals; feelings; moral decisions; and such concepts as freedom, justice, love, labor, autonomy, commitment, and democracy, which others communicate (Mezirow, 1990). In turn, I honed these skills through critical self-reflection, affirming Mezirow's transformation theory of adult learning (1990) as requiring a process of reflection, reassessment, and interpretation of assumptions on which we base our beliefs. Learning online was therefore a complex process. I was learning by doing, interacting with others, and constantly self-reflecting on (and making meaning of) my experiences in cyberspace, while reassessing my own orientation to learning in general.

My experience as an online learner was also powerful, in that it changed how I saw myself as an adult learner and educator. It became the lens through which I focused my studies and practice as a trainer/consultant on online teaching and learning after being an online learner. Moreover, my experience was part of a transformational learning process that was not an independent act but an interdependent relationship with my classmates (Baumgartner, 2001).

My Contextual Approach to Learning in Cyberspace

According to Caffarella and Merriam (2000), the contextual perspective of adult learning is grounded in a sociocultural framework. This means that "learning cannot be separated from the context in which the learning takes place" (p. 59). Therefore, a contextual approach to learning is based on interactive (learning as a product of the individual interacting with the context) and structural (the influence on learning of such social and cultural aspects as race, class, gender, ethnicity, and power and oppression) dimensions (Caffarella and Merriam, 2000).

Interactive Dimension. Situated cognition and reflective practice are two examples of learning that encompasses the interactive contextual framework. In the adult education literature, Hansman and Wilson (1998) define situated cognition as "a relationship between the individual and the social or physical situation in which he or she learns. Knowing, from a situated cognition perspective, is not just an independent internal mental process, but is fundamentally situated as a product of activity, context, and culture." Caffarella and Merriam (2000) suggest that situated cognition can be integrated into the learning process by using a highly sophisticated simulation of real-life activities and events.

Moreover, reflective practice allows learners "to make judgments in complex and murky situations, judgments based on experience and prior knowledge" (Caffarella and Merriam, 2000, p. 60). Reflection-in-action is used to facilitate the interactive reflective mode because it helps learners complete a task through a process that allows them to reshape what they are working on, while they are working on it (Schön, 1987).

Both situated cognition and reflective practice were suitable approaches for my learning in cyberspace. When instructional strategies focused on situated cognition, as an online learner I was often sharing my cultural background with classmates during the online discussion of a topic. For me, this was a way to make sense of my own experience through clarifying it for others. I was interpreting new concepts through culture-specific conceptual frameworks of meaning (Jacobson, 1996). My classmates were also learning about my culture from a situated perspective from my writings.

In cyberspace, I recognize that the instructional design of the online environment (the graphical user interface of the course management tool) has a great influence on the interactive dimension of learning. The instructional design of a course is based on the instructional strategies (activities the learner will perform during the duration of a course), human interactions (exchanges between instructor and learner, learner and learner, learner and guest participant), nonhuman interactions (exchanges between learner and content, learner and tools, and so forth), and evaluation (instructor feedback and strategies for individual assessment of tasks and self-evaluation). This means the opportunity to gain knowledge and interact with other learners is dependent on the design of the online course. A course that offers a space for interaction with other participants, critical reflection of assumptions, and analysis and interpretation of concepts allows me to validate my beliefs, intentions, values, and feelings.

Structural Dimension. Social and cultural factors such as gender and national origin had an impact on the outcome of my learning experience in cyberspace. As a woman raised in a conservative society, I found that the online environment gave me the sense of a safe place for intellectual growth through psychological and interpersonal support while I was going through significant changes in my worldview (Burge, 1998). My perceptions of behavioral norms of a woman in Brazil included being a listener and nurturer, rather than a critical thinker. By contrast, living in the United States, experiencing a more female-empowered environment, hearing the stories of other women, and sharing my own stories all helped me to critically reflect on my assumptions about gender and gave me a new perspective on what it meant to be a woman in society. Expressing my ideas about gender issues and reflecting on my perspective in an environment free of face-to-face encounters were an emancipatory act.

Being born and raised in a conservative area of Latin America, I held assumptions about learning that were characterized by a teacher-centered approach with the design of instruction controlled by the instructor and learner performance influenced by the consent of the authority figure. My participation in adult education courses, and particularly online instruction, challenged this view. In cyberspace, the online learning design and implementation focused on a learner-centered approach, which prevented reinforcement of the instructor power position and affirmed and used the cultural experiences and knowledge of all class members.

What is more important, having the opportunity to facilitate online discussions and moderate chats helped me build my self-confidence and leadership skills. Participation through the written word as opposed to the spoken word improved my ability to perform tasks and roles relative to those of my classmates as well. I felt I had a voice that was recognized and validated when others made comments reflecting on my postings.

Cyberspace was an appropriate environment for me to positively experience the process of acculturation within the culture of America's higher education. I was open for change, and the environment allowed me to express ideas and reflect on assumptions in a way that was safe. The new learning experience challenged my way of thinking and helped me develop new learning skills. Being challenged, I broadened my repertoire of learning styles, which prepared me to function in today's society. My experiences as an online learner demonstrated that the individual and contextual perspectives are interconnected. Linking these two perspectives in exploring the learning experiences helped me gain a better understanding of the multitude of contexts that have shaped and continue to shape my learning as an adult and my practice as an adult educator.

Implications of Learning and Teaching in the Context of Cyberspace

In this chapter, I have used the individual and contextual perspectives addressed in the adult education literature to guide exploration and sharing of my experiences as an adult learner in cyberspace. These experiences can serve to make us more aware of what it means for an individual to learn in cyberspace and how context can shape the learner and learning transactions (Caffarella and Merriam, 2000). The accounts of my online experiences are not to be overgeneralized, however. Rather, together with other experiences presented in this volume, they may yield insights into the influence of sociocultural factors on individual and group learning.

Learning online brings new challenges and suggests new ways of thinking about adult education practice. It is my belief that as adult educators, we need to look at each learning situation carefully because learners represent a variety of backgrounds, gender experiences, and learning styles. Therefore, it is important to consider differences across diverse groups of learners in designing and delivering online courses effectively. One must also consider the increased number of ethnic minority groups in the United States as having an additional impact in the educational system (Sanchez and Gunawardena, 1998). Accommodating more ethnic minority members as learners might well prepare us for using the Internet to reach an even more diverse learner population successfully.

Social and culturally relevant adult education in cyberspace requires self-awareness and knowledge of the learner's background, interests, and level of experience. Instructional strategies such as sharing biographical information and stories, experiential learning and reflection, journaling, asynchronous and synchronous discussion, collaborating on course assignments, problem solving, critical thinking, and analyzing and evaluating information can help educators design an environment that can meet the needs of diverse learners in cyberspace (Hanna, Glowacki-Dudka, and Conceição-Runlee, 2000).

Awareness of the way diverse learners communicate, behave, and think can help the adult educator develop a course more effectively. Being aware of learning styles and how the context can shape the learner and the learning transactions has major implications for course design and learner support. Giving learners a variety of instructional activities and resources using online technologies can allow them to succeed in a way that may challenge and help them expand their learning style to better function in a diverse society.

References

Baumgartner, L. "An Update on Transformational Learning." In S. B. Merriam (ed.), *The New Update on Adult Learning Theory*. New Directions in Adult and Continuing Education, no. 89. San Francisco: Jossey-Bass, 2001.

Burge, E. "Gender in Distance Education." In C. C. Gibson (ed.), *Distance Learners in Higher Education: Institutional Responses for Quality Outcomes*. Madison, Wis.: Atwood, 1998.

Caffarella, R. S., and Merriam, S. B. "Linking the Individual Learner to the Context of Adult Learning." In A. Wilson and E. Hayes (eds.), *Handbook of Adult and Continuing Education*. San Francisco: Jossey-Bass, 2000.

Clark, M. C. "Transformational Learning." In S. B. Merriam (ed.), *An Update on Adult Learning Theory*. New Directions in Adult and Continuing Education, no. 57. San Francisco: Jossey-Bass, 1993.

Conceição-Runlee, S., and Reilly, K. "Experiences of Faculty Members Who Interact with Students in an Online Environment." In A. Austin, G. E. Haynes, and R. T. Miller (eds.), *Proceedings of the Eighteenth Annual Midwest Research-to-Practice Conference in Adult, Continuing, and Community Education*, University of Missouri, St. Louis, Sept. 22–24, 1999.

Garrison, D. R. "Self-Directed Learning: Toward a Comprehensive Model." *Adult Education Quarterly*, 1997, 24 (1), 18–33.

Hanna, D., Glowacki-Dudka, M., and Conceição-Runlee, S. *147 Practical Tips for Teaching Online Groups: Essentials of Web-Based Education*. Madison, Wis.: Atwood, 2000.

Hansman, C. A. "Context-Based Adult Learning." In S. B. Merriam (ed.), *The New Update on Adult Learning Theory*. New Directions in Adult and Continuing Education, no. 89. San Francisco: Jossey-Bass, 2001.

Hansman, C. A., and Wilson, A. L. "Cognition and Practice: Adult Learning Situated in Everyday Activity." In *Proceedings of the 39th Annual Adult Education Research Conference*, University of the Incarnate Word, San Antonio, May 15–16, 1998.

Hayes, E. "A New Look at Women's Learning." In S. B. Merriam (ed.), *The New Update on Adult Learning Theory*. New Directions in Adult and Continuing Education, no. 89. San Francisco: Jossey-Bass, 2001.

Jacobson, W. "Learning, Culture, and Learning Culture." *Adult Education Quarterly, 47* (1), 15–28, 1996.

Merriam, S. B., and Caffarella, R. S. *Learning in adulthood* (2nd ed.). San Francisco: Jossey-Bass, 1999.

Mezirow, J. "How Critical Reflection Triggers Learning." In J. Mezirow (ed.), *Fostering Critical Reflection in Adulthood*. San Francisco: Jossey-Bass, 1990.

Mezirow, J. "On Critical Reflection." *Adult Education Quarterly*, 1998, 48 (3), 185–198.

Sanchez, I., and Gunawardena, C. N. "Understanding and Supporting the Culturally Diverse Distance Learner." In C. C. Gibson (ed.), *Distance Learners in Higher Education: Institutional Responses for Quality Outcomes*. Madison, Wis.: Atwood, 1998.

Schön, D. A. *Educating the Reflective Practitioner*. San Francisco: Jossey-Bass, 1987.

SIMONE CONCEIÇÃO is assistant professor of adult and continuing education in the Department of Administrative Leadership at the University of Wisconsin-Milwaukee.

5

The sociocultural constructs of race, class, and gender combine with the effects of disability to create powerful influences on the educational and work history of adults with disabilities.

Sociocultural Contexts of Learning Among Adults with Disabilities

Jovita M. Ross-Gordon

As adult educators, we are already encouraged to be aware of the sociocultural contexts of our learners. The need for such awareness is no less when the learner is one with a disability. This chapter explores how the sociocultural variables of race, class, and gender interact with those of disability; it offers implications for providing programs and services for an ethnically and culturally diverse group of learners with disabilities.

The Presenting Picture

As a starting point, it is important for those working in adult, community, and workplace education to become aware of basic data on the prevalence of disabilities, the status of adults with disabilities within the worlds of education and work, and the educational practices that have typically shaped their experiences.

Prevalence of Disabilities. Of the total U.S. noninstitutionalized population in 1992, 15 percent reported some activity limitation due to a chronic health condition, which is the definition used to determine disability by the National Health Interview Survey (LaPlante and Carlson, 1996). This survey also demonstrates several relationships between prevalence of disability and other sociodemographic variables. For instance, age-adjusted prevalence (accounting for women's greater longevity) reveals males to have a slightly higher rate of disability (15.2 percent) compared to women (14.8 percent); females have a rate comparable to that of males within each ethnic group except among non-Hispanic whites. Of the ethnic and racial groups identified by this survey, Asians and Pacific Islanders had the lowest rate of disability (7.2 percent), with Hispanics showing the next lowest (10.4 percent). The survey also showed the highest rate of limitation among Native Americans (17.6 percent), for whom activity limitation was 40 percent higher than for non-Hispanic whites when age adjusted. Non-Hispanic blacks and whites appear to have similar rates at 15.9 percent and 15.8 percent, respectively, but adjusting for age (because the non-Hispanic white population is older) showed blacks with a greater prevalence (18.3 percent) than whites (14.9 percent).

Strongest predictors of disability were education, income, and age (LaPlante and Carlson, 1996). Educational attainment was highly inversely related to disability, with 38.4 percent of those with eight years or less of education reporting a disability-related limitation, a rate more than three times that of people with sixteen or more years of schooling (11.5 percent). A breakdown by income level showed a similar inverse relationship, with a ratio of three to one in prevalence of disability when those with an income of $10,000 or less were compared to those with an income of $35,000 or more. Finally, the proportion of the population with activity limitation increases with age; 56.6 percent of those eighty-five and older reported some activity limitation.

The Schooling Experience: Special Education or Lack Thereof. Many adults with a disability that dates to childhood have been influenced as learners by encounters with the special education system. Although the outcomes have been positive for many, for others negative experiences dominate their recollection. Other adults have been shaped as learners by the system's failure to identify their disability, leaving them without the educational intervention that might have led to more successful learning. Experiences of either type may be a critical part of the learning history of the adult with a disability.

Race and Ethnicity as Predictors of Participation. Mitchell (1997) offers data on implementation of the Individuals with Disabilities Education Act (IDEA), supporting long-held claims that the percentage of blacks and Hispanics in special education is higher than in the general population, while Asian American and Native American children are often underrepresented. For instance, African Americans constitute 12 percent of elementary and secondary enrollment but 28 percent of total enrollment in special education (Mitchell, 1997). Although special education placement is intended to provide a more successful schooling experience, 50 percent of minority special education students in large cities drop out of school anyway (Mitchell, 1997).

Human elements in the referral-and-assessment process appear to play a significant role in the ethnically disproportionate placement rate. Coulter (1996) reports that sixty-two of sixty-six local education agencies showed disproportionate representation of African Americans in what he termed "socially determined" disabilities (learning, emotional or behavioral, and mental) and a substantially lower representation in "biologically determined" disabilities (orthopedic, deaf, visually impaired). Similarly, using nationally representative data from former Head Start participants, Cluett and others (1998) found that different sources of information and criteria for functional impairment significantly altered the rate of identification of children with emotional and behavioral disabilities (EBD). Teachers using weighted criteria to rate behaviors and social skills tend to identify African Americans at a higher rate, but parents judging the same behaviors and skills tend to produce results that more closely resemble clinic results. Patton and Townsend (1999) raise questions about the role of ethics, power, and privilege in school practice leading to overrepresentation of minority children in special education and alternative education programs and parallel underrepresentation in gifted and talented programs. Pointing to an "ever-widening social, cultural, and economic chasm that exists between educators and their students," Patton and Townsend (1999, p. 282) suggest that misinterpretation of social and communicative behaviors related to expression of cultural identity may play a significant role in such oppressive school practices.

Gender as a Correlate of Identification. Evidence also indicates that proportionate differences in special education on the basis of gender, long held to be due to genetic, biological, or developmental differences, are actually strongly influenced by social and cultural conditions. Caseau, Luckasson, and Kroth (1994) found that although girls constituted a small proportion (21 percent) of students identified by the public schools as having a serious emotional disturbance, they made up a majority (55 percent) of the group served in a program for adolescents with emotional problems in a local hospital and referred by private therapists (55 percent). These girls had serious problems of depression, family conflict, and suicide attempts but were less likely to exhibit the kind of external behavior problems that led to school referral (disruptive class behavior, academic failure, defiance, and truancy). Conversely, McIntyre and Tong (1999) postulate that cross-gender misunderstanding between female teachers and male students can greatly affect the educational process and may result in boys who display strong traditional male behavior patterns being labeled emotionally or behaviorally disordered when they are not. They suggest boys from lower socioeconomic status are at greatest risk because of the more extreme level of "male behavior."

Young, Kim, and Gerber (1998/1999) cite two decades of accumulated evidence of gender bias in identification of learning disabilities, indicating that males have no greater statistical chance of LD despite the fact that the LD population served by public schools is 72 percent male. School-referred LD samples are more likely to have behavior problems than research-based samples, suggesting that girls, who are less likely to be disruptive in the classroom, are more likely to be overlooked. Citing studies linking unidentified LD in females with teen pregnancy, school dropout, and welfare participation, Young, Kim, and Gerber (1998/1999) posit that the consequences of underidentified LD among females can be long-term and far-reaching. They recommend that adult programs take measures to account for lost time and opportunity among women with previously unidentified LD.

The Impact of Disability on Adults. The impact of living with a disability can be seen in multiple arenas of adult life. As with children and youth, race and ethnicity and gender appear to be related to differential outcomes among the disabled.

Participation in Services and Programs as a Function of Disability Status. Kaye (1998) reports that following implementation of ADA, the rate of labor force participation for those with disabilities remained more or less constant from 1990 to 1994 at 52 percent, while the gap in full-time wages between disabled men and their nondisabled peers actually increased during this time period. On the other hand, he reports a significant increase following ADA in the employment rate of those with severe functional limitations, rising from 27.6 percent in 1991 to 32.2 percent in 1994.

Jans and Stoddard (1999) provide data on participation in other aspects of adult life, including lower marriage rates (68 percent for women and 69 percent for men with no functional limitations) and parenting rate (30 percent of disabled adults eighteen to sixty-four). They add, "Compared to parents with no disability, parents with a disability were found to be economically and educationally disadvantaged, reporting lower incomes, higher rates of public assistance, higher high school drop-out rates, and lower college attendance" (Jans and Stoddard, 1999, p. 32). Disabled parents are also more likely to have a spouse with a disability and to have a child with a disability.

Gender, Disability Status, and Participation in Services. Lichtenstein (1996) reviewed several studies pointing to gender-related patterns in the adult outcomes of former special education students, including the National Longitudinal Transition Study, which tracked eight thousand students formerly enrolled in special education programs. On the basis of this review, he concluded that (1) young women experience a longer period and higher rate of unemployment and underemployment than their male counterparts, and (2) their experiences also differ from female peers in the general population in that among the latter the gap in employment between young women and men narrowed with time while the gender gap widened among young adults with disabilities. He further concluded that school programs chosen by or provided to many young women with disabilities support a postschool path involving home and child care more actively than postsecondary education or employment.

Data from Jans and Stoddard (1999) indicate that such a trend in gender-related labor force participation continues through later adult years, with disabled women less likely to be employed, more likely to earn lower wages, more likely to live in poverty, less likely to get SSI benefits, and more likely to earn lower SSI benefits than men. Surprisingly, the gap has actually increased since 1970.

Race and Ethnicity, Disability Status, and Participation in Services. Giles (1992) notes that although blacks and Hispanics represented a growing proportion of adults with work-related disabilities during the 1980s, whites represented a slightly increasing proportion of cases rehabilitated. He cites previous studies indicating that blacks were more likely to be found ineligible for vocational rehabilitation and to take longer to be accepted than whites, were less likely to be rehabilitated if found eligible, and were less likely to receive education or training. Johnson (1991) similarly reports that although American Indian and Alaska Natives have a higher rate of disability than the general population, they are underrepresented in the service delivery system of vocational rehabilitation.

Schmidt, Curtis, and Gregg (1996) share results of a survey of eighty-three respondents that included professionals from the fields of special education and vocational rehabilitation. Asked to rank the most important problems facing African American adolescents and adults with LD, the respondents ranked these five as most frequent: (1) assessment, (2) cultural insensitivity of service providers, (3) economic barriers, (4) negative perceptions of the African American community, and (5) culturally irrelevant instructional materials. Asked their perception of the adequacy of services available to this group, 57 percent responded that available services were not adequate, while 63 percent answered that educational options are not adequate.

The literature on the status of adults with disabilities generally portrays a picture of individuals with disabilities affected by unemployment or underemployment, reduced likelihood of participation in postsecondary education, and lower participation in marriage and parenting. Gender, race, and the severity of the disability appear to be related to diminished outcomes in one or more life roles. Furthermore, racial minorities and women appear less likely to receive certain benefits such as education and training sponsored by vocational rehabilitation and SSI benefits.

Reframing the Subject

Implicit in the discussion of youth and adults with disabilities presented to this point has been an interventionist perspective based on a medical model of disability. This perspective reflects the two fields that generated the status quo described here: special education and vocational rehabilitation. It is also consistent with how the Americans with Disabilities Act (ADA) defines disability: as a physical or mental impairment that substantially limits one or more major life activities of an individual. More recently, however, the social, cultural, and political dimensions of disability have come to the fore.

Disability Studies. Much of the impetus for reconceptualizing disability has come from the emerging field of disability studies. The field has its roots in the disability rights movement of the latter half of the twentieth century, but for the most part it "came of age" in the form of academic units of study in the 1990s. What's more, professionals concerned with the interdisciplinary nature of disability take more of an interactionist perspective. Adrian cites Davis and Linton (1995): "This new focus suggests that disability issues are more social than medical, more political than individual. Emphasis is placed on how society determines disability and how the definition of disability influences the societal response to people with disabilities. More specifically, the challenge of disability studies within this broader context is to dispel the notion that the status afforded to individuals with disabilities is an outcome of their condition. Rather, the expectations for people with disabilities are an outcome of each society's view of and response to difference, including disabilities" (Adrian, 1997, para. 3).

The scholarly work of disability studies has come primarily from the liberal arts more than other fields, with significant leadership coming from scholars with disabilities (Peters, 2000; Pfeiffer, 1993; Zola, 1993) even though the disabled are largely absent from the academy (Linton, 1994). For instance, a number of university teachers have designed courses taking an interdisciplinary approach to disabilities in society, and several have described such courses in teacher education journals (Adrian, 1997; Linton, 1994; Linton, Mello, and O'Neill, 1995). However, curriculum and scholarly writing on disability in adult, community, and workplace education do not yet reflect this new perspective in any significant way.

Disability Rights and Self-Determination. Concurrent with the emergence of a sociopolitical analysis of disability has come greater interest in the legal and personal rights of the disabled. Several key pieces of legislation, most notably Section 504 of the Rehabilitation Act of 1973 and the ADA, have afforded greater rights to the disabled in the arena of education (Pfeiffer, 1993). Central to the discussion of personal rights has been emphasis on self-determination. Hence ADA requires that reasonable accommodations be made once a disability is disclosed, to allow the individual with a disability to demonstrate his or her learning or to perform required job functions.

Equal access, as supported by ADA, can certainly be seen as one of the essential conditions for self-determination for individuals with disabilities. Yet self-determination has proven to be an elusive concept to define overall. Wehmeyer (1998) differentiates the construct of self-determination into two dimensions: personal (having to do with controlling one's own life) and political (the right of a people to self-governance). Particularly with respect to the severely disabled, Wehmeyer cautions against misinterpreting self-determination—for example, to require independent performance, absolute control, or consistently successful behavior. Indeed, the most severely disabled may require assistance from others in performing even the most basic of life tasks; yet they are no less capable of self-determination.

Other authors address the political connotation of self-determination through discussion of empowerment and leadership by individuals with disabilities. Abery and Sharpe (1995) note that many changes beneficial to those with disabilities have resulted from leadership by the disabled. To avoid a leadership vacuum, they call for a broader vision of leadership on the assumption that each person has the potential to lead. However, developing this potential requires greater effort than perpetuating systems that foster dependence. Bolden (1995) cautions that even where special efforts exist to foster leadership development among the disabled, some individuals with disabilities may face additional barriers to developing leadership capacity because of bias related to race and gender. To solve these problems, she suggests service providers and advocacy groups ask specific questions about who is being excluded and develop explicit strategies to be inclusive in leadership development efforts.

Culture and Disability. Those who view disability as socially constructed recognize that that there are strong ties between culture and disability. For instance, a disability in one culture may not be viewed as such in another. Correspondingly, numerous factors shape a given culture's response to disability, including the culture's tolerance of difference. More recently, the notion of a culture of disability has come to the fore. In this view, the notion of disability is one of group belonging and distinction from other groups who do not share the disability identity (Gilson and Depoy, 2000). Although some, such as McCune (2001), have questioned whether there is one common cultural experience that supports the notion of a disability culture, others such as Peters (2000) argue that such a culture clearly has emerged. Even those who question the existence of one culture common across various disability groups are likely to acknowledge the existence of specific disability cultures, for example. One frequently mentioned example of a specific disability culture is Deaf culture. Tucker (1998) distinguishes the usage of deaf (with a small *d*) to describe those who are impaired in ability to hear but assimilated into hearing society from the usage of Deaf (with a capital *D*) to describe those who see deafness as a cultural identity they wish to maintain and nourish. The protection of Deaf culture and American sign language was the rallying cry for Gallaudet University students who protested in 1988 for the appointment of the first deaf president of that well-known university for the deaf (Shapiro, 1993). More recently, Deaf pride has surfaced in debates over whether to provide surgical cochlear implants to young deaf children before they have had an opportunity to acquire their "first" language—American sign language (Tucker, 1998). This perspective obviously views disability as part of human variability rather than as a deficit.

Implications for the Practice of Adult, Community, and Workplace Education

Relatively little literature aimed toward, and authored by, adult and continuing educators has specifically addressed the educational needs of those with disabilities (Gadbow and DuBois, 1998; Jordan, 1996; Ross-Gordon,

1989; Polson and White, 1999; Vogel and Reder, 1998). It should come as no surprise, then, that a recent federal and state agency focus group meeting on literacy needs of adults with disabilities indicated in its report that adult education providers do not fully understand the implications of ADA and Section 504 of the Rehabilitation Act for adult literacy programs ("Disability and Literacy," 1998). This finding is of significant concern given that a disproportionately high percentage of individuals in every disability group performed at level one on the 1992 National Adult Literacy Survey ("Disability and Literacy," 1998). Educators' poor understanding of their needs therefore precludes their offering the effective instruction that the disability community in all sectors of adult, community, and workplace education require.

As this chapter explains, our challenge as educators is to enhance our understanding of disability, disability rights, and the legal implications of our programs. We must also broaden that understanding to consider sociocultural dimensions of disability. This review explains a number of implications relevant to adult, community, and workplace education. Whether designing a program within basic adult education, higher adult education, the workplace, or the community, we need to recognize that:

- Adult learners bring educational histories colored by their race, gender, and economic status as well as by the sociocultural meanings attached to their visible or invisible disabilities.
- Many adults with disabilities are acutely in need of appropriate education and training strategies and accommodations, given educational histories that may include misidentification or lack of identification of their disability and work history that often includes unemployment and underemployment.
- All adults possess learning abilities that can serve as the basis for identifying appropriate accommodations to enable them to demonstrate their potential in learning and work. Adults themselves are likely to be the best partners in identifying appropriate and reasonable accommodations.
- Because of past exposure to dependency-fostering educational and service practices, adults with disabilities may not be well prepared initially to exercise the level of self-determination and leadership of which they are capable.
- As instructors, trainers, administrators, and advocates, we often bring assumption and bias related to disability, acquired through our own sociocultural experiences, into our teaching. Part of our work, then, must involve becoming aware of bias and revising it.

Additionally, building on the knowledge presented here, several principles for action in program development can be suggested. For instance, we should:

- Offer and participate in professional development opportunities designed to increase awareness of legislative mandates having an impact on the education of adults with disabilities (Rothstein, 1998).
- Create learning and work environments that move beyond mere tolerance of difference on the basis of disability, race, class, and gender to promote full inclusion and social justice.
- Actively seek to enhance awareness among educational colleagues and employers of various types of disability—physical and mental, visible and invisible—as well as sociocultural interpretations of racial, cultural, and disability groups.
- Create learning and work environments that maximize the potential of all by using accommodations and assistive technologies creatively. To do so, we should capitalize on the self-awareness and experience of learners with disabilities.
- Create environments that foster self-determination and empowerment of individuals with disabilities, rather than dependence and compliance.

Although it may take some time for our efforts to produce tangible results, it is important that we start immediately to improve our level of awareness and the responsiveness of our programs to the diverse needs of adult learners with disabilities.

References

Abery, B., and Sharpe, M. N. "Leadership Persons with Disabilities: Perceptions, Needs, and Opportunities." *Impact,* 1995, *8* (3), 21–30.

Adrian, S. E. "Disability, Society and Ethical Issues: A First-Year Experience for University Students." *Intervention in School and Clinic,* 1997, *32,* 178–84.

Bolden, J. A. "The Impact of Gender and Race on Leadership by Persons with Disabilities." *Impact,* 1995, *8* (3), 4–7. (ED 386 875)

Caseau, D. L., Luckasson, R., and Kroth, R. L. "Special Education Services for Girls with Serious Emotional Disturbance: A Case of Gender Bias?" *Behavioral Disorders,* 1994, *20* (1), 51–60.

Cluett, S. E., Forness, S. R., Ramey, S. L., Ramey, C., Hsu, C., Kavale, K., and Gresham, F. M. "Consequences of Differential Diagnostic Criteria on Identification Rates of Children with Emotional or Behavioral Disorders." *Journal of Emotional and Behavioral Disorders,* 1998, *20* (1), 51–60.

Coulter, W. A. "Alarming or Disarming? The Status of Ethnic Differences Within Exceptionalities." Paper presented at the Annual Convention of the Council for Exceptional Children, Orlando, Apr. 1996. (ED 394 297)

"Disability and Literacy: How Disability Issues Are Addressed in Adult Basic Education Programs. Findings of National Focus Group." Washington, D.C.: National Institute for Literacy, 1998. (ED 427 187)

Gadbow, N., and DuBois, D. A. *Adult Learners with Special Learning Needs: Strategies and Resources for Postsecondary Education and Workplace Training.* Malabar, Fla.: Krieger, 1998.

Giles, F. "The Vocational Rehabilitation of Minorities." In *The Unique Needs of Minorities with Disabilities: Setting an Agenda for the Future* (conference proceedings), Jackson, Miss., May 6–7, 1992. (ED 348 592)

Gilson, S. F., and Depoy, E. "Multiculturalism and Disability: A Critical Perspective." *Disability and Society,* 2000, *14* (2) 207–218.

Jans, L., and Stoddard, S. *Chartbook on Women and Disability in the United States: An InfoUse Report.* Washington, D.C.: National Institute on Disability and Rehabilitation, 1999. (ED 432 079)

Johnson, M. J. *American Indians and Alaska Natives with Disabilities.* Washington, D.C.: Rural Education and Small Schools Clearinghouse, 1991. (ED 3395 88)

Jordan, D. *Teaching Adults with Learning Disabilities.* Malabar, Fla.: Krieger, 1996.

Kaye, H. S. *Is the Status of People with Disabilities Improving?* Washington, D.C.: National Institute on Disability and Rehabilitation Research, 1998. (ED 421 824)

LaPlante, M., and Carlson, D. "Disability in the United States: Prevalence and Causes, 1992." In *Disability Statistics Report.* Washington, D.C.: National Institute on Disability and Rehabilitation Research, 1996.

Lichtenstein, S. "Gender Differences in the Education and Employment of Young Adults." *Remedial and Special Education,* 1996, 7 (1), 4–120.

Linton, S. "Reshaping Disability in Teacher Education and Beyond." *Teaching Education,* 1994, *6* (2), 9–20.

Linton, S., Mello, S., and O'Neill, J. "Disability Studies: Expanding the Parameters of Diversity." *Radical Teacher,* 1995, *47,* 4–10.

McCune, P. "What Do Disabilities Have to Do with Diversity?" *About Campus,* 2001, *6* (2), 5–12.

McIntyre, T., and Tong, V. "Where the Boys Are: Do Cross-Gender Misunderstandings of Language Use and Behavior Patterns Contribute to the Overrepresentation of Males in Programs for Students with Emotional and Behavioral Disorders?" *Education and Treatment of Children,* 1999, *21* (3), 321–332.

Mitchell, M. "Ethnicity in Special Education: A Macro-Level Analysis." (Project ALIGN issue brief.) Richmond, Va.: Donald Oswald Commonwealth Institute for Child and Family Studies, Jan. 1997. (ED 408 770)

Patton, J. M., and Townsend, B. L. "Ethics, Power and Privilege: Neglected Considerations in the Education of African American Learners with Special Needs." *Teacher Education and Special Education,* 1999, *22* (4), 276–286.

Peters, S. "Is There a Disability Culture: A Syncretisation of Three Possible World Views." *Disability and Society,* 2000, *15* (4), 583–601.

Pfeiffer, D. "Overview of the Disability Movement: History, Legislative Record, and Political Implications." *Policy Studies Journal,* 1993, *21* (4), 724–734.

Polson, C. J., and White, W. J. "Accommodations for Adults with Disabilities in Adult Basic Education Centers." *Adult Basic Education,* 1999, *9* (2), 90–103.

Ross-Gordon, J. M. *Adults with Learning Disabilities: An Overview for the Adult Educator.* ERIC Information Services no. 337. Washington, D.C.: Office of Educational Research and Improvement, 1989. (ED 315 664)

Rothstein, L. F. "The Americans with Disabilities Act. Section 504, and Adults with Learning Disabilities in Adult Education and Transition to Employment." In S. A. Vogel and S. Reder (eds.), *Learning Disability, Literacy, and Adult Education.* Baltimore: Brookes, 1998.

Schmidt, S. F., Curtis, R., and Gregg, N. "Introduction: Multiple Factors Impacting the Assessment and Instruction of African American Adolescents and Adults with Learning Disabilities." In N. Gregg, R., Curtis, and S. F. Schmidt (eds.), *African American Adolescents and Adults with Learning Disabilities: An Overview of Assessment Issues.* Washington, D.C.: National Institute on Disability and Rehabilitation Research, 1996. (ED 415 629)

Shapiro, J. P. *No Pity: People with Disabilities Forging a New Civil Rights Movement.* New York: Times Books, 1993.

Tucker, B. T. "Deaf Culture, Cochlear Implants, and Elective Disability." *Hastings Center Report,* 1998, *28* (4), 6–14.

Vogel, S. A., and Reder, S. *Learning Disabilities, Literacy and Adult Education.* Baltimore: Brookes, 1998.

Wehmeyer, M. L. "Self-Determination of Individuals with Significant Disabilities: Examining Meanings and Misinterpretations." *Journal of the Association for Persons with Severe Handicaps,* 1998, *23* (11), 5–16.

Young, G. H., Kim, H. J., and Gerber, P. J. "Gender Bias and Learning Disabilities: School Age and Long Term Consequences for Females." *Learning Disabilities,* Fall 1998/Winter 1999, *3,* 107–114.

Zola, I. K. "Self, Identity and the Naming Question: Reflections on the Language of Disability." *Social Sciences and Medicine,* 1993, *36* (2), 167–173.

JOVITA M. ROSS-GORDON is associate professor of education administration and psychological services at Southwest Texas State University, where she teaches in the master's program in developmental and adult education and the doctoral major in adult, professional, and community education.

6

This chapter proposes a rationale for shifting the predominant adult literacy education model of decontextualized and monologic programs to a sociocultural approach. Such an approach takes into account the functions of literacy as a cultural practice within social relations in a particular social context.

Adult Literacy as Cultural Practice

Barbara Sparks

Recent discussion of the hostile climate toward immigrants and passage of English-only laws in the southwest remind Mexican American adults of being punished for speaking Spanish in elementary school. As one man explained, "At school we weren't allowed to speak Spanish. If you got caught you would get in trouble—couldn't get recess, had to stand in the corner. I don't know if it was right, but it worked. We learned English" (Eduardo, quoted in Sparks, 2002).

At the same time, women on welfare around the United States struggle to acquire education and training in preparation for employment that will pay them a living wage. Many recipients see preparing for the GED exam as necessary since vocational training, though it might give them some marketable job skills, is typically for low-skill, low-wage work. One woman chanted that when she applied for jobs they always wanted the "GED, GED, GED."

Finally, older Laotian refugees gladly go to daily English classes month after month even though they have little expectation of gaining sufficient skill to handle the literacy demands of their new country. One man described the lessons as a social event, like going to market! (Wikelund, 1989).

These people share not only low-level skills in English literacy but also awareness of the social context in which they function and understanding of the social value of literacy skills in that context. Furthermore, how they understand the social aspects of literacy affects their behavior regarding acquisition and use of literacy skills. Literacy, then, is a cultural practice dependent on the functions it serves and the social relations within varying social contexts.

Adult literacy classes, adult basic education (ABE), and English as a second language (ESL) attract people primarily from two distinct but related groups: relative newcomers from third-world countries and U.S.-born peoples whose economic and social lives have much in common with what is encountered in third-world countries. Each broad category of adult learner brings its own unique, socially constructed cultural practices, feelings, history, and knowledge to these classes.

On the other hand, the emphasis on the functional needs for adult social roles and individual growth drives the literacy effort. Because of functional concerns, decontextualized literacy programs using skills-based textbooks and materials assigned by teachers according to state or federal guidelines and assessments dominate adult literacy education (Purcell-Gates, Degener, and Jacobson, 1998). Moreover, dominant social and political interests intervene in defining content, direction, and prevailing values in the literacy curriculum. Current research and practice define literacy for children within a sociocultural context (Perez, 1998; Gee, 1992; Zanger, 1994), but adult literacy education has not benefited from the debate over authentic literacy activity rooted in the life reality of learners or their context-based interests and expertise. Practice, then, is lagging far behind theory.

I propose a sociocultural approach to understanding adult literacy, which takes into account how literacy is acquired and used in social interaction within a situational context. I then move on to some of the conflicts in adult literacy practice as divergent cultural and political interests converge. Finally, I discuss implications for literacy education practice.

Adult Literacy as Culture

Adult literacy education, from a sociocultural perspective, recognizes contextualized cultural forms of literacy, including the social relations of active agents interacting with other active agents and locally produced meaning within a specific context. In discussing the relationship between literacy and culture, Ferdman (1991) states that "each of us maintains an image of the behaviors, beliefs, values, and norms—in short, of the culture—appropriate to members of the ethnic groups(s) to which we belong" (p. 348). Every literacy user is a member of a defined culture with a cultural identity that "both derives from and modulates the symbolic and practical significance of literacy" (p. 348). For example, in the early 1990s the ethnically diverse southwestern United States struggled with English-only legislation. Spanish-speaking indigenous groups viewed English-only as a threat to their cultural identity, while the dominant, elite, English-speaking groups contended that a monolingual citizenry was necessary for a unified nation. Another example is the distinction that can be made between the literacy practices of poor women, who most often use oral tradition for sharing parenting information, and the literacy practices of middle-class women, who rely heavily on parenting experts and printed materials. In other words, the degree to which people engage in learning or using literacy is a function of their cultural identity and the symbolic and practical significance of literacy in their particular sociocultural context.

Raymond Williams, a cultural theorist and an adult educator of the British working class, defines "culture as the signifying system through which. . . . a social order is communicated, reproduced, experienced and explored" (1981, p. 13). This signifying system is seen as essentially involved in all forms of social activity and is a distinct "whole way of life" (p. 13). It includes not only belief systems, institutions, and explicit relationships but also "a social experience which is still in process, often indeed not yet recognized as social but taken to be private, idiosyncratic, and even isolating, but which in analysis has its emergent, connecting, and dominant characteristics" (Williams, 1977, p. 132). He describes this set of defining characteristics as "structures of feeling" (p. 128).

Rather than using the concept of a worldview or a group outlook, which Williams sees as rooted in experience, the concept of structures of feeling moves beyond experience to include dynamic and interactive forms of thought and being that influence contextualized meaning. Thus, although people use literacy to achieve their goals in a variety of contexts, culture as a whole way of life is a determining influence in deciding what is to be done or not done in expressing oneself; the structures of feeling dictate what is learned. Culture is the set of social processes of introspection, social interaction, and formation of relations, as well as the product itself (language, artifacts, rituals, and institutions, as they are constituted through culturally specific practices and relations). This reciprocal relationship creates the distinctive culture of a particular class or group and, by extension, a particular ethnic, gender, sexually oriented, or geographic group.

Further, Williams wants "to find other terms for the undeniable experience of the present" (1977, p. 128), beyond the temporal present with its institutions, formations, and positions as a fixed product (such as a literacy text or ABE program), as well as its defining product (such as social conventions of formality or seniority). He focuses on what is "defined as the personal: this, here, now, alive, active, 'subjective'" (p. 128). He sees literacy as a formative cultural process within a specific present, such as the emergent socializing culture of spoken word poetry events where youths use popular culture to speak about their lives as they learn the rhythms and layering of metaphor for social critique (Dimitriadis, 2001; Sparks and Grochowski, 2002). This emphasis of culture as the "experience of the present" contrasts with the common tendency to think of cultural experience as an already completed process or product of memory, a thing already in existence like a speech pattern or form of address. Culture, then, is an act of becoming that is formative and forming.

People's use of literacy skills is socially constructed to respond to shifting and dynamic circumstances. Monkman (1997) tells of the transnational sociocultural context of Mexican and Honduran adult literacy experiences. As they participate in social networks in their home country and in their new community in California, language and literacy abilities often become shared resources (see also Fingeret's work, 1983). The role within a social network sometimes determines who learns and uses which skills. As transnational network dynamics and relations are transformed over time and in different locales, so too are learning and literacy experiences reshaped and redefined.

For instance, the use of literacy by street youths as discussed by Wikelund (1989) is often a social activity. Interacting as a group, they deal with written materials, joking and interpreting the meaning of magazine articles, want ads, assistance forms, and crossword puzzles among other things. Working together, some contribute bits of functional knowledge about the item and the consequences of its use, while others offer technological literacy skills in the form of reading and writing.

The cultural event of literacy as social practice is also evident in the informal learning among welfare mothers who gather to discuss the contents and ramifications of their self-sufficiency contract (Sparks and MacDaniels, 2001). These examples illustrate the social consciousness of the individuals and their understanding of the social acceptability of writing and reading in daily life. As active subjects interacting with the cultural processes of literacy, they are continuously creating and reformulating specific literacy practices and texts to accommodate a particular and situated present.

Notice the historically distinct quality of Williams's comment (1977) as well. He states that "we are defining a particular quality of social experience and relationship, historically distinct from other particular qualities which give the sense of a generation or of a period" (Williams, 1977, p. 131). He goes on to say that this social experience of literacy is "a specific structure of particular linkages, particular emphases, and suppressions, and particular deep starting-points and conclusions" (p. 134). This marks changing institutions, beliefs, and formations within dynamic social relationships. As change in "structures of feeling" occurs, we are concerned with the shift in meaning and values as they are actively lived and felt, and the relations between these and formal or systematic beliefs about literacy.

To take an example, let us consider Wikelund's comparative study (1989) of an Eskimo fishing village; a community of Hmong immigrants; and a partially migrant, partially settled Hispanic community. Each encountered rapidly increasing demands for literacy in everyday life yet was historically distinctive, unique, and illustrative of the historical shifts in structures of feeling. In the Eskimo village, literacy increasingly penetrated village life, introducing new concerns from the outside world and changing the relationships between the village and external governmental agencies. These changes accelerated the transition of villagers from subsistence fishing to commercial fishing. As a result, new demands for literacy skills were increasingly imposed upon the adult community. The Hmong community, in contrast, were transplanted from their traditional environment and economy in Southeast Asia to a radically different setting with incremental demands for new language and literacy skills. Finally, in the Hispanic community some adults had already developed English literacy skills in Mexico while others became literate in a new language in the new environment.

These examples represent various sociohistorical contexts that can influence the interactional dynamics of literacy acquisition. The sociohistorical context relates to a set of internal relations at once interlocking and in tension, as well as in relation between people and systems. An understanding of history as an ongoing stream of human action and thought, at the nexus of what can and cannot be changed, is determined by historical actors themselves and offers a possible interpretation of the politics of literacy within the United States (Demetrion, 1998).

Value and Conflict in Literacy Practice

A look at the socially determined meanings that cultural groups give to literacy processes and products leads to the necessity of recognizing "the complex relation of differentiated structures of feeling of differentiated groups" (Williams, 1977, p. 134). Thus literacy cannot be considered to be content-free or context-free; it is a system of skills, values, and ways of thinking learned in a specific setting; it is always used in service of, or filtered through, the culture and cultural identity. However, literacy as a cultural practice only becomes social consciousness when it is lived, actively, in a relationship that is more than a systematic exchange between fixed entities. Williams (1977) argues that "there are frequent tensions between the received interpretation and practical experience. . . . Practical consciousness is almost always different from official consciousness, and this is not only a matter of relative freedom or control. For practical consciousness is what is actually being lived, and not only what is thought is being lived" (p. 130–131).

Differentiated structures of feeling signal issues of power differential and the tension between various cultural groups. Which culture is of more value becomes problematic, especially for members of a nondominant group. Because of variation in cultural forms of thought and subsequent cultural interaction, individuals struggle for understanding of, and participation in, mainstream culture but may not have the cultural repertoire to navigate and negotiate a cross-cultural environment or situation. This holds true for dominant group members as well, who may be monocultural and lack the ability to navigate multiple cultural borders.

Knowledge, then, is a specific function of literacy, such as using literacy to gain services; as a result it varies according to the cultural group and the social context (the doctor, the family, a store). In a study of Mexican Americans and literacy (Sparks, 2002), one woman told of how she asked the store clerk to write out her checks when paying for groceries; another talked of how he translated conversation between a Spanish speaking coworker and the English-speaking boss on the construction site. By contrast, consider the work of Gumperz (1982), which shows the cultural dissonance in cross-cultural interaction. He presents the example of an interview between an East Indian job applicant and English-speaking interviewers. The exchange of greetings, a basic and seemingly transparent encounter, becomes a problematic beginning to a completely failed interview. Operating from a different cultural perspective, the interviewee got fewer and fewer clear cues as to what was expected of him. The man had to rely on the English-speaking interviewers, participants in the official culture that determined and regulated the interview process.

All of these incidents reflect the tension between the practical consciousness of lived reality and the determining influence of the dominant language, or the official consciousness. There is a "culture of power" (Delpit, 1988, p. 282) at work that contains codes or rules relating to "linguistic forms, communicative strategies, and presentation of self; that is, ways of talking, writing, dressing and interacting." Delpit further suggests that the rules of the culture of power reflect the rules of the culture *of those who have power.* Most significant for our purposes, these dominant and hegemonic criteria and their norms and evaluations are reproduced in the classroom or in general society through discourse practices (Zuss, 1994). By looking at the value differences of various discourse communities, we can see another view of the tension between unequal linguistic exchange and distribution of power; literacy practices are embedded in and negotiated between discourse communities.

The notion of the discourse community emerges from ethnographic studies of communication from the 1970s. Gee (1992) argues that discourse is acquired to deal with everyday life within a sociocultural context that is part of a larger communicative societal system or sociopolitical entity. A discourse community organizes and legitimates particular forms of knowledge and social practices at the expense of others. Some examples are the privileging of standard English over black English or the southern white dialect; the preference for printed text over oral tradition; and the assimilation of nonnative English speakers into the dominant language. There is debate about the determinism of discourse theory (Delpit, 1993; Purcell-Gates, 1995), but the norms of the discourse community determine not only production of text, convention, speech forms, and vocabulary but also socioculturally distinctive and integrated ways of acting, talking, writing, interacting, and valuing connected with a particular social identity or role.

As adult educators, therefore, it is vital that we critically reflect on the social relations established by the privileged modes of discourse in the cross-cultural classroom. The reason for this is obvious. The culture of power points to teacher authority and the principles and guiding premises of curricula and textbooks serving as the official structure of feeling that maintains educational standards, methods, and content.

Furthermore, as stated previously, the majority of adult literacy programs address literacy from a decontextualized, monologic, and privileged position; this position is in conflict with the lived reality of the cross-cultural classroom (Purcell-Gates, Degener, and Jacobson, 1998), resulting in a clash of cultural texts. But this is not all. As Perez (1998) states, "Learners assume an active role of creative participation" (p. 25). Furthermore, according to Zuss (1994):

> What must be emphasized and supplemented to [Delpit's] notion of power is its dynamic quality as an interactive relation in which students in cross-cultural encounters are not merely acted upon, but act in opposition or resistance to dominant forms of the culture of power. Discourse communities and subcultural group identities cohere; their resilience is based on shared experience and knowledge. Even the kind of voluntary subcultural groupings that may arise during the span of a semester—such as working women with children, or individuals studying together for civil service or academic testing—have the capacity, at least potentially, to act as autonomous agents in formulating their own standards, goals, and forms of value and power. [p. 244]

The point here is that as active creative participants in various subcultures, adult learners bring with them already formed and forming cultural literacy practices. In a complex, pluralistic society, subcultures are in transition and in dynamic relationship with other cultures. As Demetrion tells us, "What is important, then, is not so much the preservation of certain subcultural practices and values as a universal matrix frozen forever in time, but the ability of individuals, groups and subcultures to reconstruct their cultures in ways that lead to self-defined progress" (1998, p. 83). This is a hopeful idea, but most adult literacy instructors seem unwilling or unable to incorporate a learner's prior life experience into instructional material and practice. Therefore, despite substantial documentation (Fingeret, 1991) of the powerful role of context in learning and the adult student's desire for such a contextualized program, the promise of the research remains largely unfulfilled.

Even if learners can reconstruct their culture through an adult literacy program in a way that truly leads to self-defined progress, Williams's research (1977) suggests another potential conflict, that of conflicting forms of thought between learners' multiple discourse communities and the official classroom discourse transmitted through literacy education. A complicating factor that many teachers are unaware of are the cultural foundations of literacy in their own lives as well as the lives of others, since as members of the mainstream culture they have been trained within a linguistically and socially homogeneous profession. Consequently, they have not learned to value forms of learning that are situated outside the traditional Eurocentric paradigm.

Necessary Steps for a Sociocultural Literacy Practice

What does all of this mean for an adult literacy program? Several things. First, a sociocultural approach to adult literacy requires understanding the social meaning of literacy. Szwed (cited in Wikelund, 1989) defines the sociocultural approach to literacy as "the roles these abilities [reading and writing] play in social life; the varieties of reading and writing available for choice; the contexts for their performance; and the manner in which they are interpreted and tested, not by experts, but by ordinary people in ordinary activities" (p. 116). Since curriculum development is crucial to teaching, the teacher needs to know about the learner's culture, not simply as a reified artifact like food, clothing, or entertainment, but as a form of thought, being, and relationships.

Two incidents come to mind that clarify this point. When I first started teaching in an adult literacy program in Milwaukee's Mexican American neighborhood, I started learning Spanish. As I struggled with the language, one of my students told me that even though it was important for me to learn Spanish, it was more important for me to understand *what it represented:* the values, the meanings, the relationships it established. Years later, I began researching Mexican American experiences with adult literacy programs in the southwestern United States. In talking about the restricted use of Spanish in ESL classes, one woman told me that Spanish was her whole life, it was who she was, it was her identity. She didn't feel it was fair for teachers to ask her to forget who she was just because she wanted to improve her English (Sparks, 2002). She wanted her cultural self-identity to be legitimized.

Florio-Ruane and Raphael (1999) are teacher educators who design professional development events; a master's course called Culture, Literacy, and Autobiography; and a voluntary book club for teachers to learn about culture. Their premise is that that members of the dominant culture hold "taken for granted assumptions of an amorphous monoculturalism and a stance of color blindness. This social positioning limits their reflection upon and discussion of race, racism, and whiteness" (p. 5). Through the use of narrative and biography (reading about the lives of others and writing about their own learning history), teachers explored identity and power at the individual and the group level. The literature afforded the opportunity to compare and contrast people's experiences in historical periods, societies, gender roles, and social location as well as across cultural landscapes. Teachers learned that elements of culture were nested in accounts of family history and intergenerational transformation. Such interventions have the potential to transform knowledge about cultural identity, and to help put teachers in touch with alternative ways of being (forms of thought) as well as other means of literacy development and use in a specific sociocultural context. With this knowledge, a program can be restructured to more closely reflect the lives of diverse learners and their needs.

Educators must critique their underlying assumptions about their philosophy and approach to teaching adults. My contention is that one of the reasons Purcell-Gates, Degener, and Jacobson (1998) found so many adult literacy programs to be monologic and decontextualized is the intentional, as well as unintentional, promotion of assimilation. I agree with Monkman (1997), who contends that any assimilationist program must make clear its intention and goals so that learners can choose whether their goals match those of the program. If, by contrast, educators are interested in meeting students where they are and create a meaningful, cultural learning experience, they should have open discussion that can lead to a dynamic and collaborative program. Literacy learners must have access to an education that they help shape and that builds upon their cultural experiences and structures of feeling.

References

Delpit, L. "The Silenced Dialogue: Power and Pedagogy in Educating Other People's Children." *Harvard Educational Review*, 1988, *58* (3) 280–298.

Delpit, L. "The Politics of Teaching Literate Discourse." In T. Perry and J. W. Fraser (eds.), *Freedom's Plow*. New York: Routledge, 1993.

Demetrion, G. "A Critical Pedagogy of the Mainstream." *Adult Basic Education*, 1998, *8* (2), 68–90.

Dimitriadis, G. *Performing Identity Performing Culture: Hip Hop as Text, Pedagogy, and Lived Practice*. New York: Peter Lang, 2001.

Ferdman, B. Literacy and Cultural Identity. In M. Minami and B. Kennedy (eds.), *Language Issues in Literacy and Bilingual/Multicultural Education*. Cambridge, Mass.: Harvard Educational Review, 1991.

Fingeret, A. "Social Network: A New Perspective on Independence and Illiterate Adults." *Adult Education Quarterly*, 1983, *33* (3), 133–146.

Fingeret, A. "Meaning, Experience, Literacy." *Adult Basic Education*, 1991, *1* (1), 1–11.

Florio-Ruane, S., and Raphael, T. *Culture, Autobiography, and the Education of Literacy Teachers*. Ann Arbor: University of Michigan, 1999.

Gee, J. P. *The Social Mind: Language, Ideology, and Social Practice*. New York: Bergin and Garvey, 1992.

Gumperz, J. J. *Language and Social Identity*. Cambridge: Cambridge University Press, 1982.

Monkman, K. "Transnational or Immigrant Learners: Redrawing the Boundaries of Sociocultural Context in Understanding Adult Learning." Paper presented at the annual meeting of the Comparative and International Education Society, Mexico City, Mar. 19, 1997.

Perez, B. "Language, Literacy, and Biliteracy." In B. Perez (ed.), *Sociocultural Contexts of Language and Literacy*. Mahwah, N.J.: Erlbaum, 1998.

Purcell-Gates, V. *Other People's Words: The Cycle of Low Literacy*. Cambridge, Mass.: Harvard University Press, 1995.

Purcell-Gates, V., Degener, S., and Jacobson, E. *U.S. Adult Literacy Program Practice: A Typology Across Dimensions of Life-Contextualized/Decontextualized and Dialogic/Monologic*. Cambridge, Mass.: National Center for the Study of Adult Learning and Literacy, 1998.

Sparks, B. *The Struggles of Getting an Education: Issues of Power, Culture, and Difference for Mexican Americans of the Southwest*. De Kalb: Educational Studies Press, Northern Illinois University, 2002.

Sparks, B., and Grochowski, C. "Narratives of Youth: Cultural Critique Through Spoken Word." Paper presented at the *IX Seminario Científico Sobre La Calidad De La Educacion: Intercambio de Experiencias de Profesionales Cubanos y Norteamericanos,* Matanzas, Cuba, Feb. 9–15, 2002.

Sparks, B., and MacDaniels, C. *Poor Women in Community Making Meaning: The Construction of Subjugated Knowledge.* Unpublished manuscript, North Carolina State University, 2001.

Wikelund, K. *Social Aspects of Literacy Acquisition and Use.* Portland, Oreg.: Northwest Regional Educational Laboratory, 1989.

Williams, R. *Marxism and Literature.* Oxford: Oxford University Press, 1977.

Williams, R. *Culture.* Glasgow: Fontana Press, 1981.

Zanger, V. "Not Joined In: The Social Context of English Literacy Development for Hispanic Youth." In B. Ferdman, R. Weber, and A. Ramirez (eds.), *Literacy Across Languages and Cultures.* Albany: State University of New York Press, 1994.

Zuss, M. "Value and Subjectivity in Literacy Practice." In B. Ferdman, R. Weber, and A. Ramirez (eds.), *Literacy Across Languages and Cultures.* Albany: State University of New York Press, 1994.

BARBARA SPARKS is assistant professor of adult education, affiliate faculty, Women and Gender Studies, Department of Adult and Community College Education, at North Carolina State University.

This chapter focuses on how the changing demographics of the U.S. workforce shape learning at work. It offers a synopsis of the changing workforce, profiles various demographic groups, and recommends a new workforce pedagogy that is sensitive to sociocultural context.

The Sociocultural Contexts of Learning in the Workplace

Laura L. Bierema

Most adults work for pay during their lifetime, making the workplace a significant context for learning (Ray and Rinzler, 1993). Organizations play an enormous role in workforce development, but they may be inhospitable to learning, seeking goals that fail to serve the learner. Moreover, each organization and worker is unique. Each has values, cultures, identities, and social norms that coalesce into the complex sociocultural system of work. This chapter explores how the changing demographics of the U.S. workforce shape learning at work. It offers a synopsis of the changing workforce, profiles various demographic groups, and recommends a new workforce pedagogy that is sensitive to sociocultural context.

The Changing U.S. Workforce

The U.S. Census Bureau predicts dramatic demographic shifts over the next one hundred years. The population is expected to grow slowly and age rapidly, while immigration increases (Little and Triest, 2002). Aging workers, women, people of color, gays and lesbians, immigrants, and religious groups populate the workplace today, but even though these groups have a significant impact on work context, they do not represent every category of diversity in the workplace.

Aging Population. The U. S. Census Bureau predicts that the population over age sixty-five will rise from its current 13 percent to 23 percent by 2100 (Little and Triest, 2002). However, despite this demographic trend, a recent study conducted by the National Council of Aging found persisting ageist views in more than 50 percent of employers (Reio and Saunders-Reio, 1999).

NEW DIRECTIONS FOR ADULT AND CONTINUING EDUCATION, no. 96, Winter 2002 © Wiley Periodicals, Inc.

For example, the Department of Labor reports that people fifty-five to sixty-four were only one-third as likely to receive training as someone age thirty-five to forty-four, and older workers attending training were often mistreated and viewed as "untrainable" (Maurer and Rafuse, 2001). Training for the older worker is usually focused on basic skill development rather than exposure to new ideas or activities that lead to promotion and pay increase. The experience of older workers may be diminished or over-looked in an educational program since erroneous, ageist assumptions are widespread about their interest in and ability to learn. Furthermore, age eventually gives those already marginalized a double minority status and has the potential to marginalize even white men.

Despite these unsettling findings, research has shown there is no evidence of a pattern of superior performance or productivity in any age group. Adult learners perform well in their job, desire learning, are able to learn as well as younger people, and often help younger people learn. In fact, older workers outshine younger workers in loyalty, satisfaction, and attendance.

Women. Women make up nearly half of the U.S. workforce, yet they experience discrimination on the basis of position, pay, and promotion. White women, however, do fare better than women of color, who often receive lesser wages, fewer jobs, and less frequent promotions as compared to middle-class white men (Hackett and Byars, 1996). For example, Lach (1999) reports, on a Catalyst study of more than seventeen hundred professional women of color, that 47 percent feel their advancement opportunities have improved over the past five years, in comparison to 60 percent of white women. Moreover, only 22 percent felt their boss was trained to manage a diverse workforce.

It seems that women are at a developmental disadvantage in the workplace because of the hidden curriculum that teaches them how to assimilate patriarchal culture, and they have an expectation that they must suppress female identity to succeed (Bierema, 2001). Women also lack developmental relationships and access to training and other activities that aid promotion of white males.

Race. Race and ethnicity categories have increased from two (white or black) in 1860 to eighteen in the 2000 Census (U.S. Census Bureau, 2001). In fact, "minorities" are the majority in six of the eight largest U.S. metropolitan areas (Society of Human Resource Management, 2001). Yet despite the growth of racial groups, the Bureau of Labor Statistics (in Digh, 1998) reports only a slight increase in the percentage of executive, administrative, and managerial positions held by African Americans, from 6.2 percent in 1993 to 6.9 percent in 1997. Even though only one in five African Americans rates corporate America favorably for equitable promotion, 80 percent believe discriminatory practices are commonplace (Digh, 1998).

To further explore this problem, Greenhaus, Parasuraman, and Wormley (1990) examined relationships among race, organizational experiences, job performance evaluation, and career outcome for black and white managers from three organizations. They found that, compared to white managers, blacks felt less accepted, viewed themselves as having less job discretion, received lower performance ratings, were more likely to have reached a career plateau, and experienced less career satisfaction.

Obviously, racial groups face special developmental issues on account of racism and lack of equal access to training and promotional opportunity. In fact, people of color often have "double minority status," meaning they belong to two disenfranchised groups (as with lesbians or women of color). Homophobic and racist attitudes may also be expressed in a training environment, making the workplace a hostile one for learning, especially for these double-minority members.

Sexual Orientation. A Society for Human Resource Management survey found at least 10 percent of the workforce is gay or lesbian, and another survey of fourteen hundred gay men and lesbians in Philadelphia showed that 76 percent of men and 81 percent of women concealed their orientation at work (Digh, 1999). Sexual orientation, whether it is heterosexual, homosexual, or bisexual, is not chosen, although this is a common misconception. It is therefore inappropriate to refer to sexuality as a "choice," "preference," or "lifestyle" when discussing it in work or other context (Digh, 1999). *Sexual orientation* is the appropriate terminology. Thus discrimination against workers on the basis of sexual orientation is a civil rights issue. Although not protected under Title VII, sexual orientation falls under the spirit of "protected class," as defined by the law that protects other immutable characteristics such as age, race, ethnicity, sex, and national origin.

Despite this legal protection, a gay or lesbian worker still faces developmental issues caused by workplace hostility, harassment, and less access to promotion and developmental programs than a heterosexual colleague. Furthermore, even those who conceal their orientation to avoid these problems suffer the developmental consequences caused by this suppression of identity.

Immigration. Contrary to predicted population declines, early 2000 Census results indicate that the U.S. population grew by 13.2 percent between 1990 and 2000, reaching 281 million. The surge in Hispanic population accounted for nearly half of this unexpected gain (Little and Triest, 2002; U.S. Census Bureau, 2000), and data from the Immigration and Naturalization Service (INS) indicate that immigrants may have accounted for approximately 35 percent of the U.S. population growth and about 40 percent of growth in the labor force since the mid-1960s (Little and Triest, 2002).

The composition of the immigrant group has changed from Europeans to people of Latino and Asian descent. Furthermore, a predicted two billion young people live in developing countries, and it is predicted that two-thirds of new entrants into the global workforce will come from the developing countries (Graig, Haley, Luss, and Schieber, 2002). Given these facts, it is clear that the resultant increased immigration raises at least two issues for an organization to address: language and religion.

Language. In 1990, approximately fourteen million foreign-born U.S. residents indicated they had limited or no English language proficiency. Since then, over five million more legal immigrants have immigrated; additionally, the population of illegal immigrants is greater than five million, a 28 percent increase since 1992, according to the INS (Digh, 1998). From 1980 to 1990, the number of people speaking languages other than English increased from 23.1 million to 31.8 million, and Spanish is now the most common non-English language spoken in the nation, followed by French, German, Italian, and Chinese (Digh, 1998).

Despite this increasingly multilingual American reality, U.S. courts have consistently maintained that Title VII does not protect workers' ability to express their cultural heritage (such as speaking a native language) in the workplace and that conversing on the job in any language is allowed at the employer's discretion (Digh, 1998). In fact, some organizations have adopted an English-only policy claiming business necessity, a practice the ACLU (American Civil Liberties Union, 2002) considers anti-immigrant. They suggest that "English-only rules corrode civil liberties and foster bigotry and intolerance" (in Digh, 1998, p. 4). However, no federal law specifically prohibits or supports English-only rules, provided they do not have a disparate impact on race or nationality. Thus far, twenty-three states have passed English-only laws, which only one state has overturned (Arizona, in April 1998) as a violation of federal constitutional rights.

Religion. New demographic patterns are changing the religious composition of the workforce. Since religion is a core aspect of identity, this new religious diversity in the workplace is quickly becoming a civil rights issue that could affect the bottom line of the business world. Immigration from Africa, Asia, and the Middle East, for instance, is adding Muslims, Buddhists, and other non-Judeo-Christians to the workplace. These newcomers to the workforce bring spiritual beliefs and practices that are relatively unknown in the U.S. workplace culture. Furthermore, older workers, who tend to be more religiously observant, are staying in the workforce past retirement or returning from retirement (Bennett, 2001), exacerbating the problem.

The U.S. workplace is inundated with Christianity, yet few people notice how entrenched it is in calendars and holidays. Few Christians have to take a personal day to observe Christmas, for example, but Hindus, Jews, and Muslims are not so fortunate and are also often forced to work on their observed Sabbath when it falls on a day other than Sunday.

According to the EEOC (Equal Employment Opportunity Commission, 2001), complaints of religion-based bias have increased almost 59 percent since 1992. In fact, a national survey of 675 workers about religious bias at work in 1999 revealed that 20 percent reported experiencing or knowing of religious bias in their workplace (Bennett, 2001). The percentage increased when respondents were asked if employees were prevented from taking time off work to observe a religious holiday, afraid to ask for time off to observe a religious holiday, not allowed a break for prayer time, harassed due to religious beliefs, told they were not to wear any type of beard or facial hair or any type of head covering—even for religious reasons, not promoted as quickly as other employees on the basis of clothing or expression of faith, or dismissed for expressing religious views through dress.

Bennett (2001) argues that few companies are prepared to address religious diversity and very few (less than 19 percent in 1997) included religion in diversity or management training. Furthermore, only 15 percent of employers make available space or time for religious observance, and only 13 percent accommodate the needs of any religion other than Christianity. Resultant developmental issues for immigrants include pressure to suppress cultural heritage; exclusion from developmental programs on the basis of English proficiency; and less access to promotion because of religious belief, dress, or practices.

New Workplace Pedagogy

If you are not a white male in the U.S. workplace, chances are you may have less access to training and development programs, receive fewer promotions, suppress your identity to assimilate to a patriarchal culture, and experience harassment or other mistreatment. If English is not your first language, you are likely to be excluded from developmental programs and may be forced to suppress your cultural or religious heritage—even if you are an English speaker—to keep your job or receive a promotion. Since none of these dynamics fosters learning and development in the workplace, we require new thinking and action to address sociocultural issues at work.

Workplace educators need to be brave about arguing for workers' ownership and control in the workplace (Spencer, 2001) and to take responsibility for ethical workplace education in a socioculturally rich context. Addressing sociocultural development within the work context depends on exploration of cultural dimensions and assumptions about difference in the workplace, to help workers recognize cultural identity and challenge workplace management of that identity (Fenwick, 2001). Because the workplace is the only context where the worker has the opportunity to learn about and develop vocational knowledge, the need for developing a workplace pedagogy is becoming evident (Billett, 2001; Bradford, 1999).

We must embrace a new workforce pedagogy, grounded in the critical management studies (CMS) tradition (Elliott and Turnbull, 2002), that challenges organizational practices that "are generally understood to be devoted to the [scientific] improvement of managerial practice and the functioning of organizations" (Alvesson and Willmott, 1992, p. 1). Workplace learning and development is often performance-based; management-driven; and sometimes damaging to an adult's sense of identity, self-worth, and control because it attempts to be culturally neutral. The proposed new workplace pedagogy challenges human resource development (HRD) to move beyond concerns about performance to broader sociocultural issues.

The new workplace pedagogy departs from traditional training and development wisdom, being mindful of the need for new approaches with a diverse workforce. It involves linking the individual and the context, reconceptualizing workplace development as a lifelong process, formulating socioculturally sensitive policy, providing equal opportunity development, and adopting diversity and multicultural programs with a critical eye and a cautious heart.

Linking the Individual and the Context. One means of practicing more critical HRD is for workplace educators to link individual development to social context on the basis of the inseparability of the two. Caffarella and Merriam (2000) suggest that the contextual approach to learning is characterized by interactive dimensions that view learning as a result of the individual engaging with a particular context; and structural dimensions that account for social and cultural factors such as race, class, gender, ethnicity, power, and oppression.

Linking individual and context requires educators to question power dynamics in the learning setting to assess whether and how power should be shared with the learner and to reflect on what constitutes knowledge. This approach demands that educators understand learners as individuals, as well as the contextual dynamics affecting them, the educators themselves, and the learning process.

Reconceptualizing Workplace Development as a Lifelong Process. A new workplace pedagogy requires a long-term perspective on development. Thus far, no one has developed a comprehensive model of the career development of racial and ethnic minorities; almost no one has explored the intersection of gender and ethnic influences on career self-efficacy, particularly among women (Farmer and Associates, 1997; Hackett and Byars, 1996; Schrieber, 1998); and few have studied the needs of older workers, which often remain invisible.

Organizations interested in retaining and sustaining workers at all ages must rethink learning and career development as a lifelong process, not just a one-shot developmental program for the young at the start of their career. The organization must also recognize that developmental needs differ with the sociocultural history of the employee and are strongly influenced by work context.

Adult educators and HRD professionals must increase their awareness of "-isms" influencing the workplace across the lifespan and help educate people about the consequences of a damaging stereotype. Educators can also model positive attitudes and respect toward diverse learners; give them voice in the learning situation; correct damage done by ageist, sexist, or racist educators; and challenge the organization to promote policies and practices of equitable thought and behavior.

Formulating Socioculturally Sensitive Policy. Laws do exist to protect people from discrimination on the basis of sex, race, age, and religion. Although these laws do not explicitly discuss sexual orientation and language, the spirit of the laws (if not the actual letter) certainly suggests that they too be prohibited as a basis for discrimination in the workforce. Despite this, many organizational policies are inherently sexist, ageist, racist, heterosexist, or Eurocentric. Therefore, workplace educators must work with organizational managers to challenge these practices, developing nondiscriminatory policies and making job training and assignment decisions neutrally.

Although gays and lesbians are not legally protected from discrimination, many U.S. organizations have adopted an equal opportunity policy, indicating they will treat sexual orientation like the other legally protected categories of race, sex, color, religion, national origin, and disability. An organization can also take several policy steps to create an environment supportive of gay and lesbian employees: extending benefit programs to include domestic partners; advocating for legal change; establishing a nondiscrimination policy on the basis of sexual orientation; educating all employees about sexual orientation; and creating a workplace where all individuals are free from discrimination, hostility, and harassment (Digh, 1999).

As previously stated, religious policies are often Eurocentric and Christian. Employers are legally required to avoid discrimination on the basis of religion; to accomplish this, they must adopt more flexible policies. Unfortunately, the policies they do adopt fall short of creating a hospitable environment for the religiously diverse. Employers and educators can go further by modeling and demanding respect for religious diversity and adopting a policy of no tolerance for any form of bias or prejudice.

Providing Equal Opportunity Development. Workplace development opportunities are not created equally. Women, people of color, gays and lesbians, older workers, and non-English speakers have less access to developmental opportunity leading to higher pay and promotion. They are all left on their own to forge an identity in a white, male-dominated, Eurocentric world that values youth and heterosexuality.

The organizations must provide training and development more equitably and assess who is attending the programs that lead to higher pay and promotion. To this end, educators have a responsibility to take inventory of the demographic make-up of participants in an educational program and to address nonrepresented groups with management. Non-English speakers are particularly disadvantaged because they are excluded from training or have limited ability to understand it. The organization should hire supervisors who speak the language of non-English speaking workers, offer English classes and incentives for learning English, and also offer non-English-language classes and incentives for English-speaking employees to learn other languages.

Adopting Diversity Programs with a Critical Eye and a Cautious Heart. The American Society for Training and Development's 2002 State of the Industry Report ranked diversity as the second most prevalent concern of HRD professionals (VanBuren and Erskine, 2002), yet diversity training may falsely raise expectations, reinforce stereotypes, and create resentment among the employees it is designed to help.

The dominant diversity discourse heralds pluralism and multiculturalism, and it is generally believed that celebrating diversity is universally good. Nevertheless, Malik (2001) argues that the problem with embracing diversity and multiculturalism is that it celebrates *difference*. He notes that "the idea of difference has always been at the heart, not of the antiracist, but of the racist agenda; and the creation of a 'multiculturalist' society has been at the expense of a more equal one" (p. 32). He explains further: "The promotion of multiculturalism is a tacit admission that the barriers that separate Blacks and Whites cannot be breached and that equality has been abandoned as a social policy goal. . . . America is not multicultural; it is simply unequal" (p. 33). Campaigning for equality involves challenging accepted practices and policies, going against the grain, and seeking social transformation (Malik, 2001). Merely celebrating diversity, by contrast, "allows us to accept society as it is—all it says is 'we live in a diverse world, enjoy it,' allowing us to accept the divisions and inequalities that characterize the world today" (Malik, 2001, p. 34). Malik concludes that only in an equal society does difference have any meaning, since only in an equal society can difference be freely chosen.

Conclusion

The U.S. workforce is diverse and changing. Organizations and educators must respond to these changes through adopting a new workplace pedagogy that links the individual and context, reconceptualizes workplace development as a lifelong process, formulates socioculturally sensitive policy, provides equal opportunity development, acts to foster change, and adopts diversity and multiculturalism programs with a critical eye and a cautious heart.

Although workers differ, developmental programs that overemphasize difference may fail to address ways of promoting equality among employees. A better approach would be to "understand an organization as a rich and complex world of relationships rather than as a set of positions" (McDaniel and Walls, 1997, p. 366). Relationships among a diverse workforce are more complex than among homogeneous groups. Diverse organizations succeed at sociocultural issues when their managers and educators embrace heterogeneity; involve workers in decisions at all levels; acknowledge and work with (rather than oversimplify) the complexity of the systems; and communicate richly, multidirectionally, and dialogically.

References

Alvesson, M., and Willmott, H. (eds.). *Critical Management Studies*. London: Sage, 1992.
American Civil Liberties Union. "The Rights of Immigrants: No. 20." Retrieved June 1, 2002. (www.aclu.org/library/pbp20.html)

Bennett, G. F. "Religious Diversity in the Workplace: An Emerging Issue." *Diversity Factor*, 2001, 9 (2), 15–20.

Bierema, L. L. "Women, Work and Learning." In T. Fenwick (ed.), *Sociocultural Perspectives on Learning Through Work*. New Directions for Adult and Continuing Education, no. 92. San Francisco: Jossey-Bass, 2001.

Billett, S. "Co-Participation: Affordance and Engagement at Work." In T. Fenwick (ed.), *Sociocultural Perspectives on Learning Through Work*. New Directions for Adult and Continuing Education, no. 92. San Francisco: Jossey-Bass, 2001.

Bradford, P. "Workplace Learning: Developing a Holistic Model." *Learning Organization*, 1999, 6 (1), 18–29.

Caffarella, R., and Merriam, S. B. "Linking the Individual Learner to the Context of Adult Learning." In A. L. Wilson and E. R. Hayes (eds.), *Handbook of Adult and Continuing Education*. San Francisco: Jossey-Bass, 2000.

Digh, P. "Race Matters." *Mosaics: Society of Human Resource Development*, 1998, 4 (5), pp. 1ff.

Digh, P. Can't Anyone Here Speak English?" *Mosaics: Society of Human Resource Development*, 1999, 4 (6), 1, 4–7.

Elliott, C., and Turnbull, S. "Critical Thinking in HRD—A Panel Led Discussion." In T. M. Egan, and S. Lynham (eds.), *Proceedings of the 2002 Academy of Human Resource Development Conference*, Honolulu, Feb. 27–Mar. 3, 2002.

Equal Employment Opportunity Commission. "Religion-Based Charges, FY 1992—FY 2001." Accessed Feb. 6, 2002. (www.eeoc.gov/stats/religion.html)

Farmer, H. S., and Associates. *Diversity and Women's Career Development: From Adolescence to Adulthood*. Thousand Oaks, Calif.: Sage, 1997.

Fenwick, T. "Tides of Change: New Themes and Questions in Workplace Learning." In T. Fenwick (ed.), *Sociocultural Perspectives on Learning Through Work*. New Directions for Adult and Continuing Education, no. 92. San Francisco: Jossey-Bass, 2001.

Graig, L., Haley, J., Luss, R., and Schieber, S. J. "The Perfect (Demographic) Storm: The Impact of a Maturing Workforce on Benefit Costs." *Compensation and Benefits Management*, 2002, 18 (1), 16–26.

Greenhaus, J. H., Parasuraman, S., and Wormley, W. M. "Effects of Race on Organizational Experiences, Job Performance Evaluations, and Career Outcomes." *Academy of Management Journal*, 1990, 33 (1), 64–86.

Hackett, G., and Byars, A. M. "Social Cognitive Theory and the Career Development of African American Women." *Career Development Quarterly*, 1996, 44 (4), 322–334.

Lach, J. "Minority Women Hit a Concrete Ceiling." *American Demographics*, 1999, 21 (9), 18–19.

Little, J. S., and Triest, R. K. "The Impact of Demographic Change on Labor Markets." *New England Economic Review*, 2002, 47–68.

Malik, K. "The Perils of Pluralism: A Re-Examination of the Terms of Engagement Between Races and Cultures, and a Plea for Equality." *Diversity Factor*, Spring 2001, pp. 31–34.

Maurer, T. J., and Rafuse, N. E. "Learning, Not Litigating: Managing Employee Development and Avoiding Claims of Age Discrimination." *Academy of Management Executive*, 2001, 15 (4), 110–121.

McDaniel, R. R., and Walls, M. E. "Diversity as a Management Strategy for Organizations: A View Through the Lenses of Chaos and Quantum Theories." *Journal of Management Inquiry*, 1997, 6 (4), 363–375.

Ray, M., and Rinzler, A. (eds.). *The New Paradigm in Business: Emerging Strategies for Leadership and Organizational Change*. New York: Putnam, 1993.

Reio, T. G., and Saunders-Reio, J. "Combating Workplace Ageism." *Adult Learning*, 1999, 11 (1), 10–13.

Schrieber, P. J. "Women's Career Development Patterns." In L. L. Bierema (ed.), *Women's Career Development Across the Lifespan: Insights and Strategies for Women,*

Organizations, and Adult Educators. New Directions for Adult and Continuing Education, no. 80. San Francisco: Jossey-Bass, 1998.

Society of Human Resource Management. "What Is the 'Business Case' for Diversity?" 2001. (www.shrm.org/diversity/default.asp?page=businesscase.htm)

Spencer, B. "Challenging Questions of Workplace Learning Researchers." In T. Fenwick, (ed.), *Sociocultural Perspectives on Learning Through Work.* New Directions for Adult and Continuing Education, no. 92. San Francisco: Jossey-Bass, 2001.

U.S. Census Bureau. Population Estimates Program. Washington, D.C.: Population Division, 2000. Accessed Mar. 6, 2002. (http://eire.census.gove/popest/estimates.php)

U.S. Census Bureau. "200 Years of U.S. Census Taking: Population and Housing Questions 1790–1990." Washington, D.C.: Bureau of the Census, Department of Commerce, 2001. (www.ameristat.org/racethnic/census.htm)

U.S. Department of Labor, Women's Bureau. "Facts on Working Women: Women of Hispanic Origin in the Workforce." 1994. (www.dol.gov/dol/wb/public/wb_pubs/hisp931.htm)

VanBuren, M., and Erskine, W. *The 2002 State of the Industry Report.* Alexandria, Va.: American Society for Training and Development, 2002.

LAURA L. BIEREMA is assistant professor of adult education at the University of Georgia.

8

Although continuing professional education programs are important in general, four specific elements of the context in which professionals deliver services to clients have an especially profound influence on learning in professional practice.

Context: Implications for Learning in Professional Practice

Barbara J. Daley

> Professional knowledge cannot be characterized in a manner that is independent of how it is learned and how it is used. It is through looking at the contexts of its acquisition and its use that its essential nature is revealed."
> —Michael Eraut (1994, p. 19)

It is often assumed that to keep up-to-date in their practice professionals learn and gain information from continuing professional education programs. Although CPE programs do, in reality, play a vital role in providing new and up-to-date information to professionals, the context in which professionals practice also has a vital role in framing what professionals learn, and how they use the information they gain from a CPE program. The program and the context of practice form an integrated system that frames not only what the professional learns but also how he or she actually uses that information to provide services to clients.

How Context Affects Learning in Professional Practice

In this chapter, I discuss how the sociocultural context of professional practice affects professional learning. On the basis of the CPE literature and previous research, I believe there are four main characteristics of context that frame learning in professional practice. These characteristics influence how professionals take in new information and also constitute a lens through which the professional views situations. This view, in turn, influences how

NEW DIRECTIONS FOR ADULT AND CONTINUING EDUCATION, no. 96, Winter 2002 © Wiley Periodicals, Inc.

the professional uses new information in the context of his or her practice. There are four such characteristics:

1. Allegiance to the profession
2. Nature of professional work
3. Variations in organizational culture
4. Level of independence and autonomy

I discuss each of these characteristics; offer examples of how they affect professions such as nursing, social work, and law; and discuss how understanding them can help the adult educator develop a program for continuing professional development.

Allegiance to Profession. Professionals in today's society often function within a specific organizational context. A lawyer may practice in a large firm, in a small corporation, or in solo practice; a nurse may practice in a hospital, home care, or long-term care; and a social worker may practice in a private counseling clinic or community-based agency, to name but a few examples. In a preprofessional preparation program, learners are educated to function in a particular way, yet the context of their practice may vary a great deal. One of the issues facing the professional is how to balance the demands of the context of employment with his or her view of professional practice. Professionals often choose to align themselves with the tenets of their professional work, rather than with the organization in which they are employed.

Barley and Van Maanen (1984) increase our understanding of this phenomenon in their discussion of the *occupational community,* which they define as "a group of people who consider themselves to be engaged in the same sort of work; who identify (more or less positively) with their work; who share a set of values, norms, and perspectives that apply to, but extend beyond, work-related matters; and whose social relationships meld the realms of work and leisure" (p. 295). An occupational community is unique in that it features shared characteristics that make the people in it more similar to other members of the occupational community than to people in the rest of the organization in which they work. An occupational community exists and functions within a specific context, but the beliefs, values, and assumptions on which the community operates may come from outside that context. Jobs and work positions may be created and managed by the organization, but the larger occupational community, and not the specific organization, defines the roles, responsibilities, and behaviors of its members.

Studies I have completed (Daley, 2001a, 2001b) demonstrate that professionals view themselves as part of an occupational community, involved in the same sort of work. They identify, as did Barley and Van Maanen and for the most part positively, with the work and their clients; they share many similarities in what they know, learn and understand from their work; and they often have social relationships with others in the same community.

Barley and Van Maanen also indicate that the social identity embedded in work is important to the occupational community and central to the self-image of the individuals within that community. In fact, this self-image is socially constructed within the community from daily interactions with others in it. These social identifiers revolve around what they refer to as "tie-signs," a "complex system of codes which enable the members of an occupation to communicate to one another an occupationally specific view of the work world" (1984, p. 299).

In previous studies (Daley, 2000), professionals indicate that daily interaction with colleagues helps form this socially constructed image of themselves. This interaction also increases their allegiance to the profession. The interaction and the development of professional tie-signs have an impact on what professionals learn and how they use that information in their practice. For example, nurses and social workers indicate that their bosses and colleagues are usually open to new ideas and willing to try new things, so they feel comfortable in bringing information from CPE back to their occupational community. Nurses and social workers say they often talk with colleagues about new ideas or just run things by them before trying something they have just learned.

Lawyers, however, often work in the context of an individual or a solo practice, and as a result they use another process to develop a socially constructed image of the profession and thus employ new information in their practice. Lawyers indicate that they often have to seek out a colleague to discuss new ideas if there are not enough easily accessible colleagues with whom to talk. As a result, many lawyers have developed an informal network of colleagues with whom they can interact. Sometimes this is a lunch or breakfast group meeting infrequently when an issue arises. At other times, it might be a structured group that meets routinely. It is interesting that, although these groups are created for the express purpose of sharing ideas in practice, they are often created outside of a CPE mechanism. For example, a lawyer in a previous study described a group with which she was involved:

> There are eight or nine female attorneys that are about my age that get together once a month. It started when we all felt burned out and we had to talk to someone; since we are not in a firm, you need someone to bounce things off of. It started out being the burned out lady lawyers' luncheon. Now we are "the BOLLL." We meet at a restaurant once a month on Fridays. We interact, and maybe we will help each other. If somebody learned anything in a seminar that someone else was at or had a case that was different, we kind of bounce ideas back and forth [Daley, 2001a, p. 46].

As this lawyer indicates, it is the personal and professional colleague relationships that shaped the learning rather than the CPE program.

In summary, the content of what professionals learn in a CPE program is related to how they view themselves within their professional community and how they go about establishing professional relationships and tie-signs. If other professionals sanction, support, and affirm the learning as important in the professional role or the professional self-identity, then the information from a CPE program tends to be readily incorporated into professional work. Just as Barley and Van Maanen (1984) demonstrate, it is the opinion of the occupational community that can drive this acceptance or rejection of new knowledge.

Nature of Professional Work. The second characteristic of the context of professional practice that frames professional learning is the nature of the work itself. How professionals view what they do day to day affects what they choose to learn and how they go about learning it. As Barley and Van Maanen explain, employing an occupational perspective implies "that persons weave their perspectives on work and career from the existing social, moral, physical, and intellectual character of the work itself" (1984, p. 289). The specific components of the work have an impact on learning.

Part of what makes the nature of the work unique in professional practice is the concept of involvement, or "absorption in the symbolic nature of work so that work takes on a special significance and sets the involved apart from others who do not pursue the same livelihood" (Barley and Van Maanen, 1984, p. 300). Barley and Van Maanen (1984) believe that claimed responsibility for others is a major factor leading to involvement: "When one believes that one holds a symbolic trust, identification with an occupation is facilitated" (p. 303).

Involvement in the work is a key factor for nurses, social workers, and lawyers. These professions describe a high level of involvement in their work, which influences their self-identity as well. For example, consider how this nurse sees herself: "The idea of nursing as a career. . . . I guess that's what I really see in it for myself. This is my calling. God called me to do this." Social workers describe the same high level of involvement; for instance: "What I found out was that there is a real bond between social workers. They all feel that they are fighting the good fight and it is a really tough job." Lawyers also express professional involvement. Consider this, for instance: "One reason I wanted to be a lawyer was to have a job that means more than going to the office and going back home—in general, social justice, working for good things, having a purpose beyond just going to work."

Yet even though these professionals are highly involved in their work, nurses, lawyers, and social workers all view the nature of their work differently and this view frames their learning. Two aspects of work that seem to drive the learning in most professions are the needs of the client and the services that the professional provides.

Professionals often view the needs of their client as paramount in their learning. Lawyers strive to keep up-to-date on the latest changes in the law so they can use this information to effectively handle client cases. Nurses often attend a CPE program with a specific client in mind and a desire to learn how to provide better care for that client. Social workers often function as advocates and thus seek information to assist them in this role. When professionals provide care or services to clients, they often carry a mental "blueprint" of the client's needs; it determines what they must learn to provide continuing client services.

Additionally, the services professionals provide stimulate many of the learning opportunities in which they engage. If a lawyer decides to expand her practice, she may attend a CPE program to learn more about an area of the law. If a nurse transfers to another unit in the hospital, he might attend a CPE program to add information on this specialty to his knowledge base. If a social worker sees an increase in her caseload of a specific type of client, she may see a need to attend CPE to expand her understanding of this type of client.

As such, it is often the involvement in and nature of the actual work in which professionals engage that drive what they learn. They learn to expand services, keep up-to-date on services that can be provided to clients, add information to their understanding of their professional role, and support their involvement in their chosen profession.

Variations of Organizational Culture. A third characteristic of the context of professional practice that influences learning is variation in organizational culture. Professionals practice in a multitude of settings, and the culture of these settings and organizations frames their learning. Frost (1991) discusses organizational culture not as an all-encompassing entity but rather as one existing in an *integrated, differentiated,* or *fragmented* perspective. In the first perspective, organizational culture is highly consistent. Consensus abounds, and "cultural members agree about what they are to do and why it is worthwhile to do it" (p. 8). In a differentiated perspective, subcultures exist and organizational consensus exists only within the subcultures. Frost tells us that "at the organizational level of analysis, differentiated subcultures may co-exist in harmony, conflict, or indifference to each other" (p. 8). In a fragmented perspective, by contrast, organizational ambiguity is pervasive, no clear consensus exists, and the organization is in a "constantly fluctuating pattern influenced by changes in events, attention, salience and cognitive overload" (p. 8).

Viewing a profession as a subculture of the organization in which it is practiced seems to clarify the impact of organizational culture on professional learning since it explains the contexts in which professionals practice. Research indicates (Daley, 2001a) that lawyers appear to operate in a highly integrated fashion. Thus it seems that regardless of the context, the practice of law seems to operate from an integrated cultural perspective. There is great consistency in how lawyers see their role, little ambiguity around the duties or functions they perform, and a great deal of organizational consistency in how they view the practice of law. This seems to be the case, whether a lawyer is practicing in a one-person firm or a large corporation.

However, the organizational culture in which social workers and nurses operate is quite different, since those cultures are more representative of Frost's differentiated model (1991). As such, these professionals are consistent in how they view their role, what they learn from clients, and how they value their profession. Yet differentiation exists when the subcultures of social work and nursing conflict with other subcultures within the same organization. Conflict may erupt with other professionals within the same organization about roles, boundaries, and delivery of client services. This frequently creates ambiguity and confusion between professionals about duties, roles, and responsibilities.

The role the organizational culture plays in professional learning is evident when professionals discuss organizational politics (Daley, 2000). Lawyers seem to ignore the political issues in their integrated culture and incorporate whatever information from CPE they need in their practice. It is not that lawyers are unaware of political issues; the political issues simply do not seem to affect how they use information from such a program.

Social workers, on the other hand, are well aware of the political issues and use information from CPE programs in what they see as their advocacy role. Social workers are cognizant of both the macro and micro political issues that influence their work. But they indicate their role as advocate is political, and so they feel it imperative to understand the politics of the contexts in which they work to work in the political realm to help meet their clients' needs. In other words, "The whole thing is political; as social workers, we not only work in a therapeutic situation, but everything we do has a political basis. . . . So if you are working in an outpatient mental health clinic, what is happening with HMOs and the legislators' control over that determines what we can do with clients" (Daley, 2001a, p. 47).

In contrast, nurses literally screen out information from a CPE program if they believe the political context would prevent its use. For example, they indicate they would not even share information from a CPE program if they felt they did not have the power, money, or time to use it.

In summary, whether the organizational culture is integrated, differentiated, or fragmented determines how professionals see their roles. Furthermore, the politics of the organizational culture shapes learning and the use of information in professional practice.

Level of Independence and Autonomy. A fourth characteristic in the context of professional practice that influences professional learning is the level of autonomy and independence the professional enjoys, or the extent to which his or her practice is housed within a traditional or bureaucratic organizational system. For example, social workers either practice within a governmental agency (where organizational structures largely shape their work) or work independently as therapists and therefore have a great deal of autonomy. Nurses tend to practice mostly in a bureaucratic health care system where structure affects their professional work. On the other hand, most lawyers appear to function with a great deal of autonomy and independence. Whether working in a large firm or a small one, it seems there is little impact of corporate structure on the context of a lawyer's professional practice.

How professionals function within their organizational structure is a good indicator of their autonomy and independence. Lawyers indicate that the structure of the organization has little influence on their use of knowledge. Typically (as one lawyer states), "The information that I gain when I go to those seminars has nothing to do with the actual structure of the working environment." Lawyers indicate that because of the autonomous nature of their practice, if they learn new information they want to use with a client they do so with very little concern about the structure of the firm.

Nurses, on the other hand, describe the structure of the organization as a "hurdle" and indicate that to use new information in their practice they often have to find creative ways to go around the organizational structure. For example, they describe how they often have to break rules to make sure their clients' needs are met.

Social workers seem to feel that using new information to benefit their clients is an individual responsibility. As such, they feel obligated to prevent the structure of the organization from getting in the way. These workers describe how they take information from a CPE program and use it with clients even if it means going outside an organizational policy.

So the level of independence, autonomy, and freedom the professional has to move within and around the organizational structure determines the learning and use of information in practice.

The Complex Nature of Context and Learning

So far, I have discussed four elements of the context of professional practice (allegiance to the profession, nature of professional work, organizational culture, and independence and autonomy) that affect learning. However, recent literature (Fenwick, 2000) indicates that a missing element in this framework is the individual learner and his or her unique sociocultural background. As Brown, Cervero, and Johnson-Bailey (2000) write, "The power relationships that structure social life do not stop at the classroom door. Rather, these relationships that are structured around class, race, gender and sexual orientation are also played out in all adult education classrooms and have a profound effect on all teaching and learning processes" (p. 273). However, race, class, gender, and sexual orientation of the professional and the impact that this positionality has on professional learning is an aspect of the sociocultural context of CPE that has received scant attention in the literature on context and workplace learning. For this reason, Siegel (2001) advocates considering context within professional learning, saying that both institutional components and individual agency are helpful in understanding learning in a work context. Adding individual agency and positionality to our understanding of the nature of professional learning and context increases the complex nature of this phenomenon but also adds to our ability to facilitate contextual learning in new and unique ways. Seeing this, Jeris (2001) states that "as the professions wrestle with accommodating (or excluding) more diverse new applicants to their ranks, it is imperative that incumbent professionals understand and appreciate the complex cultural issues that novices confront as they enter the professions. More importantly, it is critical to determine what CPE practitioners can do to develop new models of professional learning and development that are more culturally informed in order to retain and nurture those responsible for meeting the diverse client needs of the future" (p. 428).

Implications for the Practice of Continuing Professional Education

In this chapter, I have addressed four unique characteristics of the context of professional practice that have an influence on professional learning. This context needs to be acknowledged as a crucial consideration in providing CPE since, as Queeny (2000) relates, "Education to address application of knowledge and skills within a practice context must go beyond simply providing information and teaching technical procedures; it must help professionals build collaborative, judgmental, reflective and integrative capabilities" (p. 379). It is my belief that these four characteristics of the context of professional practice suggest three implications for providers of continuing professional education.

First, CPE providers need to base their educational programs on a fundamental understanding of the nature of professional work. This means that CPE providers must develop first-hand knowledge of the work done by those professionals for whom they are planning programs. Additionally, simple one-way transmission of information does not suffice in delivering a program. Rather, we need to develop CPE programs around actual professional practice situations so that participants have an opportunity to explore the relationship between new information being presented and their work. Experiential learning (Merriam and Caffarella, 1999), problem-based learning (Wilkerson and Gijselaers, 1996), and case-based scenarios (Lohman, 2001) all are ways to integrate a CPE program into professional work.

Second, CPE providers need to embrace the view that developing an occupational community and fostering involvement in professional work affects learning. Establishing colleague connections in professional practice is one way to assess new information while deciding if and how to use that information in practice. Thus a CPE program that promotes sharing, networking, and creating colleague relationships is not just fostering a socialization process. It is furthering professional identity development, allegiance to the profession, and tie-signs that allow professionals to communicate and discuss new information and incorporate it into their practice. Additionally, programs of this type are promoting an understanding of the individual learner and the influence of their positionality on professional learning.

Finally, CPE programs should become more attuned to adding program components to assist the professional in developing specific strategies to implement new information in the work site. These strategies need to take into consideration the organizational culture, the level of professional autonomy, and the sociocultural background and positionality of the individual learner.

In conclusion, continuous learning in professional practice requires careful integration of the CPE program and the work context. As Eraut (1994) indicates, "To make practical use of concepts and ideas other than those embedded in well-established professional traditions requires intellectual effort and an understanding of work-context. The meaning of a new idea has to be rediscovered in the practical situation, and the implication for action thought through" (p. 49). The challenge for providers of CPE programs is to foster rediscovery of new ideas in disparate practical situations.

References

Barley, S. R., and Van Maanen, J. "Occupational Communities: Culture and Control in Organizations." *Research in Organizational Behavior*, 1984, 6, 287–365.

Brown, A., Cervero, R., and Johnson-Bailey, J. "Making the Invisible Visible: Race, Gender, and Teaching in Adult Education." *Adult Education Quarterly*, 2000, 50 (4), 273–288.

Daley, B. "Learning in Professional Practice." In V. Mott and B. Daley (eds.), *Charting a Course for Continuing Professional Education: Reframing Professional Practice*. New Directions in Adult and Continuing Education, no. 86. San Francisco: Jossey Bass, 2000.

Daley, B. "Learning and Context Connections in Continuing Professional Education." In *The Cyril O. Houle Scholars in Adult and Continuing Education Program Global Research Perspectives, Vol. 1*. Athens: Department of Adult Education, University of Georgia, 2001a.

Daley, B. "Learning and Professional Practice: A Study of Four Professions." *Adult Education Quarterly*, 2001b, 52 (1), 39–54.

Eraut, M. *Developing Professional Knowledge and Competence*. London: Falmer Press, 1994.

Fenwick, T. "Putting Meaning into Workplace Learning." In A. Wilson and E. Hayes (eds.), *Handbook of Adult and Continuing Education*. San Francisco: Jossey-Bass, 2000.

Frost, P. J. *Reframing Organizational Culture*. Thousand Oaks, Calif.: Sage, 1991.

Jeris, L. "Equity and Access in the Professions: A Call for Reframing Continuing Professional Education." In P. Sawchuk (ed.), *Proceedings of the 2nd International Conference on Researching Work and Learning*, Calgary, Alberta, July 26–28, 2001.

Lohman, M. "A Comparative Analysis of Problem-Based Approaches to Professional Development." In O. Aliaga (ed.), *Proceedings of the Academy of Human Resource Development Conference*, Tulsa, Okla., Feb. 28–Mar. 4, 2001.

Merriam, S. B., and Caffarella, R. *Learning in Adulthood* (2nd ed.). San Francisco: Jossey-Bass, 1999.

Queeny, D. S. "Continuing Professional Education." In A. Wilson and E. Hayes (eds.), *Handbook of Adult and Continuing Education.* San Francisco: Jossey-Bass, 2000.

Siegel, I. "From Symbols, Stories and Social Artifacts to Social Architecture and Individual Agency: The Discourse of Learning and the Decline of Organizational Culture in the New Work Order." In R. Smith, J. Dirkx, P. Eddy, P. Farrell, and M. Polzin (eds.), *Proceedings of the 42nd Annual Adult Education Research Conference,* East Lansing, Mich., June 1–3, 2001.

Wilkerson, L., and Gijselaers, W. H. (eds.). *Bringing Problem-Based Learning to Higher Education: Theory and Practice.* New Directions for Teaching and Learning, no. 68. San Francisco: Jossey-Bass, 1996.

BARBARA J. DALEY *is associate professor of adult and continuing education in the Department of Administrative Leadership at the University of Wisconsin-Milwaukee.*

9

The literature of adult education highlights the need for educators to foster an inclusive learning environment to accommodate the multiple worldviews that learners bring. Missing from the discussion is the interplay among critical reflection of self and practice, knowledge and understanding of the problematic issues, and critical action.

Linking the Personal and the Social for a More Critical Democratic Adult Education

Mary V. Alfred

For more than a decade, adult educators have been alluding to sociocultural context as an influence on learning. For example, the earlier works of Hayes and Colin (1994); Jarvis, (1987); Ross-Gordon (1991); and Ross-Gordon, Martin, and Briscoe (1990) highlight the need for adult educators to take a multicultural approach to program planning and implementation if they are to serve the needs of their diverse constituents. More recently, the works of Alfred (2001), Amstutz (1999), Fenwick (2001), Guy (1999), Johnson-Bailey and Cervero (2000), Sheared (1994), and Tisdell (1995), among others, continue to challenge the field of adult education to be more inclusive of diverse perspectives, histories, cultures, and identities and to recognize that these contexts influence the dynamics of teaching and learning.

This plethora of literature has created the awareness that diversity matters in teaching and learning. As a result, those who center their research on issues of diversity have offered various recommendations for creating an inclusive learning environment, in the hope of making space for the multiple worldviews and perspectives that learners bring. However, these recommendations often tend to overlook the importance of critical self-awareness and development of cultural competency in building a more inclusive adult education. I argue that instructors cannot transform their practice unless they have transformed themselves.

If a facilitator is to take action in creating a more inclusive learning environment, we must first understand the problematic issues that plague our practice. In other words, not only must we be critically reflective, we must also develop the cultural competency to manage a multicultural and multiethnic learning environment. In this chapter, I present an interactive framework for developing cross-cultural competency for a more democratic adult education, drawing from the authors in this volume and from other sources.

A democratic adult education environment, therefore, is one in which a multiplicity of cultures and worldviews coexists and indeed thrives (Guy, 1999). However, as educators, we must become culturally competent to manage such a diverse learning environment. Moreover, it is important that we clear up the misconception that it is only white educators who need to develop cross-cultural competency. In fact, this challenge applies equally to all educators, across racial and cultural groups because, as Nieto (1997) points out, "We cannot assume that, simply because of their marginal status in society, African American, Latino, Asian, and American Indian prospective and practicing teachers and others different from the majority can teach students from other backgrounds. . . . Teachers from backgrounds other than European American are also largely unprepared to teach students from groups other than their own" (p. 5).

Hence, development of cross-cultural competency for a more democratic learning environment is not acquisition of a set of technical skills but rather a continuous learning process that encompasses awareness, knowledge and understanding, and action (Cox and Beale, 1997).

Awareness Through Critical Reflective Analysis

Before we can create an inclusive environment, we must acknowledge our own sociocultural histories, identities, biases, assumptions, and recognize how they influence our worldview and our interaction with members of a diverse community. Such awareness results from intense personal reflection and critical analysis of our work as practitioner or scholar. The key, here, is to balance personal transformation with the vision of critical democratic education as a continuous process of social change and transformation (Banks, 1997; Howard, 1999). This calls for adult educators to understand, decode, and dismantle the dynamics of Eurocentric dominance. As Howard notes, "if we take Cornel West's challenge to 'speak the truth to power,' then we must face our feelings of inadequacy, discomfort, and guilt. We must seek to transform both ourselves and the social conditions of injustice that continue to stifle the potential of too many of our students from all racial and cultural groups" (1999, p. 6). Linking the personal and the social transformation process begins with critical analysis of self and practice. To that end, Gerald Apps (1985) cites five reasons adult educators should remain critically reflective about their practice:

1. *Analysis helps us become aware of what we do as practitioners, including being able to see our experience in a fresh way.* Continuously seeing our

experience afresh opens space for new ideas, programs, strategies, and perspectives.

2. *Analysis shows us alternative approaches for planning and delivering programs.* As our student demographics change, it is important that we continuously analyze our programs, curricula, and design strategies to determine the extent to which we are including the diversity of perspectives that reflect the experiences of a diverse student population.

3. *Analysis helps us become aware of values, ethics, and esthetics as applied to adult and continuing education.* Ethics in adult education is often overlooked as we attempt to sustain our programs and meet institutional mandates for increased enrollment and for becoming self-sufficient. Through reflective analysis, we can see the dimensions of both ethical and unethical behavior in our practice.

4. *Through reflective analysis, we can each become aware of our own personal history and its influence on our role as an educator of adults.* As Apps notes, "much of what we are as human beings is a product of our histories, where we were born, where we grew up, where we went to school, who our friends were, who was our first lover. Who we are today is a subtle mixture of all of these forces, and they influence how we think and what we do as educators of adults" (1985, p. 7). In addition, by becoming critically reflective, we can see how our personal history informs our assumptions and influences how we plan and deliver an instructional program, and how the value we place on certain ways of knowing empowers some students and alienates others.

5. *Analysis can free us from depending on someone else's doctrine.* By becoming critically reflective, we can see how the dominant views within the literature of adult education must be expanded to allow broader perspectives and differing ways of knowing. As Apps notes, "by using analytical tools, we . . . can become autonomous individuals with the confidence to challenge and question the existing doctrines of the field and of our agencies and institutions" (1985, p. 7). Being critical about the doctrines that dominate the field does not mean we reject all existing doctrines. It simply means that we remain open to other perspectives, theories, and concepts as we build a more critical democratic adult education.

For example, in Chapter One, I sought to raise awareness of the importance of sociocultural context in adult learning. The questions presented in that chapter aimed at encouraging practitioners to reflect on their work and to broaden the philosophical assumptions that guide their practice. Encouraging students to also reflect on and articulate their experiences as adult learners can also inform transformation of our practice. For example, Conceição (in Chapter Four of this volume) demonstrated how learning within the context of cyberspace created a safe environment for her socialization into American higher education. On the other hand, Lee (in Chapter Three), another immigrant student, shared her experiences with marginalization and isolation in the traditional face-to-face classroom setting. As we reflect on our practice, we can begin to consider the individual student within his or her context of difference and determine how and what we do to empower or marginalize the student.

From the organizational perspective, diversity has been rated as the second most prevalent concern of human resource development professionals (Bierema, in Chapter Seven). As a result, organizations offer diversity programs as a way of grappling with the complexity of issues inherent in a multicultural workforce. However, in Chapter Seven Bierema cautions organizations to approach diversity programs with a critical eye and a cautious heart. Instead of promoting diversity, organizational members should promote equality by challenging taken-for-granted cultural norms and practices that disenfranchise women and minority workers.

In summary, the authors in this volume have emphasized the need for critical analysis, and the importance of educators linking personal and social transformation for improved practice. A common theme among ideas presented here is the call for us to critique our underlying assumptions about our philosophy and approach to teaching adults.

Using Knowledge to Construct and Define Alternative Solutions

Through critical analysis, we honestly name the constraints, barriers, and issues that keep us from establishing a more democratic adult education, to include our own personal histories, assumptions, and biases. Building a more critical adult education means having clear understanding of the issues and the knowledge base to choose among alternative procedures. Through reflective analysis and acquisition of knowledge, we can have a deeper cognitive grasp of how (and why it is important) to create space for diversity of ideas, worldviews, and perspectives. By creating space for such diversity, we can recognize and attempt to accommodate the myriad contexts that influence our lives and those of the learners. Multicultural competency is therefore a continuous process that incorporates reflective analysis of self and practice, a comprehensive understanding of the sociocultural contexts that influence professional practice, and the ability to choose and implement the best design and delivery strategies to foster an environment of inclusion.

The authors in this volume have researched and documented some of the sociocultural issues of adult learning and have presented information to help build the knowledge base of instructors and students alike. For example, discussion of disability issues (Ross-Gordon, Chapter Five), cross-cultural mentoring relationships (Johnson-Bailey and Cervero, Chapter Two), and immigration and adult learning (Lee and Sheared, Chapter Three) are relatively scarce in the literature of adult education, yet those contexts continue to be a site of struggle in the transformation of self and society among students and teachers alike. In Chapter Two, Johnson-Bailey and Cervero note that in their cross-cultural mentoring relationship they both armed themselves with knowledge of race and the effects of racism through readings in that area. This knowledge base helped Ron, as a white man, understand Juanita's struggles with racism in the academy. It also helped him to break the cycle of white cultural isolation that often characterizes the experience of whites (Howard, 1999). We can, as a result, suggest that to develop cross-cultural competency one must be knowledgeable of dimensions of various cultures and cultural practices and how they manifest themselves in teaching and learning. Immersing oneself in varied cultures enhances cultural competency and alleviates cultural isolation.

Similarly, with knowledge of cultures and cultural practices, we can begin to reconceptualize literacy from a monologic perspective to a more sociocultural one (Sparks, Chapter Six), thus creating an opportunity to redesign the curricula for friendlier and more relevant literacy education. Increasing our knowledge base regarding the impact of these contexts on learning allows us to make informed decisions about program planning and implementation.

Knowledge as a precursor to action must also be understood within the discourse of continuing professional education (CPE). As Daley notes in Chapter Eight, "CPE providers need to base their educational programs on a fundamental understanding of the nature of professional work. This means that CPE providers must develop first-hand knowledge of the work done by those professionals for whom they are planning programs." Discouragingly, program planning within the context of CPE has not been likely to consider the contexts of the profession or those of the individual learner in program planning.

Walking the Talk Through Reflective Action

In 1997, I listened as President Bill Clinton called for a renewed national dialogue on race. My reaction at the time was, "Haven't we done enough talking? When are we going to take real action? We seem to talk a lot about race without taking real action." As in society, adult educators have done a lot of talking about diversity in general and in our practice in particular. Many adult educators are trying to move beyond mere conversation and into action, but they are met with uncertainty and challenges that often result in part from a lack of personal awareness, knowledge, and cross-cultural incompetence. Consequently, becoming critically aware and acquiring the necessary knowledge base is critical to effective action.

Once adult educators have identified the personal and social issues that plague their practice and defined possible alternative processes, they are positioned to actually improve their delivery of adult education programs that would accommodate a more diverse community. As Wilson and Hayes (2000) emphasize, "practice demands actions." Those authors also caution that there are no rational, technical solutions for the challenges we face in the field; there are instead ambiguity, dilemma, and contradiction to which each of us must decide our own unique response, depending on the situation. As they note, "Within our historical and professional communities, we must make choices about how we understand the professional problems we face and how we will respond to them. Such judgements are rarely choices about what is unassailably 'right' and more often ambiguous dilemmas about what could be depending upon how we 'see' the situation" (p. 25). In other words, there is no defined prescription for moving to a more democratic practice. However, we must be able to identify the challenges and problems we face, we should have some knowledge about alternative solutions, and then we must choose and experiment with those that fit our unique situation. In addition, through constant reflection of self and practice we make space for creativity in constructing our own solutions to our unique challenges.

In this volume, we have offered numerous suggestions for moving to a more democratic practice. Noting that not every solution fits every situation, adult educators can select among those presented here or define their own, drawing from their knowledge base about their unique situation. Worth mentioning here is the hidden culture of disability, which forms the life world of many of our students, particularly those in adult basic education. In Chapter Five, Ross-Gordon listed several ideas to help raise awareness of the impact of disabilities, as they intersect with the structural dimensions of race, class, and gender. In addition, her recommendations for action are a start for us to begin moving the learner with a disability from outside the margin of our classroom. What Ross-Gordon is suggesting is that with the right accommodation, every adult can demonstrate the potential to learn. It is up to the instructor to develop a knowledge base on adults with disabilities and determine the necessary accommodation for those learners.

Viewing the scholarship and practice of adult education through a sociocultural lens allows us to recognize, name, and challenge hegemonic practices and ideologies, thus paving the way for a more critical democratic adult education. The process of critical awareness through reflection, enhancing understanding through knowledge, and engaging in critical action does not proceed in stages; instead, it is an interactive process of continuous transformation of the personal and the social.

References

Alfred, M. V. "The Politics of Knowledge and Theory Construction in Adult Education: A Critical Analysis from an Africentric Feminist Perspective." *MAACE Options* 2001, *13* (1), 10–20.

Amstutz, D. D. "Adult Learning: Moving Toward Inclusive Theories and Practices." In T. C. Guy (ed.), *Providing Culturally Relevant Adult Education: A Challenge for the Twenty-First Century*. New Directions for Adult and Continuing Education, no. 82. San Francisco: Jossey-Bass, 1999.

Apps, J. W. *Improving Practice in Continuing Education.* San Francisco: Jossey-Bass, 1985.

Banks, J. A. *Educating Citizens in a Multicultural Society.* New York: Teachers College Press, 1997.

Cox, T., and Beale, R. L. *Developing Competency to Manage Diversity: Readings, Cases, and Activities.* San Francisco: Berrett-Koehler, 1997.

Fenwick, T. "Tides of Change: New Themes and Questions in Workplace Learning." In T. C. Fenwick (ed.), *Sociocultural Perspectives of Learning Through Work.* New Directions for Adult and Continuing Education, no. 92. San Francisco: Jossey-Bass, 2001.

Guy, T. C. "Culture as Context for Adult Education: The Need for Culturally Relevant Adult Education." In T. C. Guy (ed.), *Providing Culturally Relevant Adult Education: A Challenge for the Twenty-First Century.* New Directions for Adult and Continuing Education, no. 82. San Francisco: Jossey-Bass, 1999.

Hayes, E., and Colin, S.A.J., III. *Racism and Sexism in the United States: Fundamental Issues.* New Directions for Adult and Continuing Education, no. 16. San Francisco: Jossey-Bass, 1994.

Howard, G. R. *We Can't Teach What We Don't Know: White Teachers, Multiracial Schools.* New York: Teachers College Press, 1999.

Jarvis, P. *Adult Learning in Social Context.* London: Croom Helm, 1987.

Johnson-Bailey, J., and Cervero, R. "Race and Adult Education: A Critical Review of the North American Literature." In T. Sork, V. Lee-Chapman, and R. St. Clair (eds.), *Proceedings of the 41st Annual Adult Education Research Conference,* University of British Columbia, Vancouver, June 2000.

Nieto, S. *Affirming Diversity: The Sociopolitical Context of Multicultural Education.* New York: Longman, 1997.

Ross-Gordon, J. M. "Needed: A Multicultural Perspective for Adult Education Research." *Adult Education Quarterly,* 1991, 42 (1), 1–16.

Ross-Gordon, J. M., Martin, L. G., and Briscoe, D. B. (eds.). *Serving Culturally Diverse Populations.* New Directions for Adult and Continuing Education, no. 48. San Francisco: Jossey-Bass, 1990.

Sheared, V. "Giving Voice: An Inclusive Model of Instruction—A Womanist Perspective." In E. Hayes and S.A.J. Colin III (eds.), *Confronting Racism and Sexism.* New Directions for Adult and Continuing Education, no. 61. San Francisco: Jossey-Bass, 1994.

Tisdell, E. J. *Creating Inclusive Adult Learning Environments: Insights from Multicultural Education and Feminist Pedagogy* (Information Series no. 361). Columbus, Ohio: ERIC Clearinghouse on Adult, Career, and Vocational Education, 1995.

Wilson, A. L., and Hayes, E. R. "On Thought and Action in Adult and Continuing Education." In A. L. Wilson and E. R. Hayes (eds.), *Handbook of Adult and Continuing Education.* San Francisco: Jossey-Bass, 2000.

MARY V. ALFRED is assistant professor of adult and continuing education in the Department of Administrative Leadership at the University of Wisconsin-Milwaukee.

INDEX

Abery, B., 52
Adrian, S. E., 52
Adult literacy, as culture, 60–63
Adult literacy program: sociocultural approach to, 66–67; two groups in, 59–60; value and conflict in, 63–65
Ageist views in the workplace, 69–70
Alfred, M. V., 11, 27, 30, 33, 89
Alvesson, M., 73
Americans with Disabilities Act (ADA), 50, 51, 52, 54
Amott, T., 29
Amstutz, D., 31, 89
Apps, G., 90, 91
Asian students and open discussions, 32–33
Assumptions, cultural, 32–33
Autonomy of professionals, 84–85

Banks, J. A., 90
Barley, S. R., 80, 81, 82
Bartolome, L., 33
Baumgartner, L., 41
Beale, R. L., 90
Bennett, G. F., 72, 73
Beyer, J. M., 5, 6, 7
Bierema, L., 2, 70, 92
Billett, S., 73
Blake, S., 20, 22
Bolden, J. A., 53
Bowman, S. R., 18, 19, 20, 22, 23, 24
Bradford, P., 73
Branscombe, N. R., 18, 19, 20, 22, 23, 24
Brinson, J., 18, 20, 21, 23
Briscoe, D. B., 11, 89
Brown, A., 85
Burge, E., 43
Byars, A. M., 70, 74

Caffarella, R. S., 4, 38, 39, 41, 42, 44, 74, 86
Carlson, D., 47, 48
Carroll, C. M., 20
Caseau, D. L., 49
Cervero, R., 1, 8, 11, 21, 22, 24, 27, 85, 89, 92, 93
Clark, M. C., 39, 41
Clinton, B., 93

Cluett, S. E., 49
Colin, S.A.J., 11, 89
Community: creating sense of, 33–34; occupational, 80–82
Conceição, S., 1, 39, 44, 91
Context(s): defined, 7; and discourse communities, 9–11, 64; as dynamic and fluid, 1, 7; importance of, 5; as sites for learning, 7–9
Contexts of learning: for adults with disabilities, 47–55; for Brazilian female, 37–44; and cross-cultural mentoring, 15–25; for immigrants, 27–34; for literacy learners, 59–67; in professional practice, 79–87; in workplace, 69–76
Continuing professional education (CPE): characteristics that influence, 79–85; suggestions for providers of, 86–87
Coulter, W. A., 48
Cox, T., 90
Critical reflective analysis, 90–92
Crosby, F. J., 19
Cross-cultural mentoring relationships: as delicate dance, 15; mentor as learner in, 22–23; personal stories of, 1, 16–17; power differences in, 22; and race, 19–22, 23–24; recommendations for, 24–25; trust in, 18–19
Cultural assumptions, examining, 32–33
Cultural discontinuity and learning, 30–31
Cultural ecology and learning, 31
Cultural models of learning, 29–30
Culture: adult literacy as, 60–63; Brazilian, 37, 43; defined, 5–6; and disability, 53; organizational, 83–84; six characteristics of, 6–7
Cummins, J., 31, 32
Cunningham, P., 16
Curriculum, inclusive, 7, 32. *See also* Democratic learning environment
Curtis, R., 51
Cyberspace learning: defined, 38; interactive dimension of, 42; motivation required for, 39; self-directed learning for, 39–40; structural dimension of, 42–43; and student diversity, 44; as transformational learning, 40–41

97

Back Issue/Subscription Order Form

Copy or detach and send to:
Jossey-Bass, A Wiley Company, 989 Market Street, San Francisco CA 94103-1741

Call or fax toll-free: Phone 888-378-2537 6:30AM – 3PM PST; Fax 888-481-2665

Back Issues: Please send me the following issues at $27 each
(Important: please include ISBN number with your order.)

_____

_____

_____

$ _____   Total for single issues

$ _____   SHIPPING CHARGES: SURFACE   Domestic Canadian
                                    First Item $5.00 $6.00
                                    Each Add'l Item $3.00 $1.50
                 For next-day and second-day delivery rates, call the number listed above.

Subscriptions: Please _start _renew my subscription to *New Directions for Adult and Continuing Education* for the year 2_____ at the following rate:

U.S.	_ Individual $70	_ Institutional $149
Canada	_ Individual $70	_ Institutional $189
All Others	_ Individual $94	_ Institutional $223
Online Subscription		_ Institutional $149

**For more information about online subscriptions visit
www.interscience.wiley.com**

$ _____   Total single issues and subscriptions (Add appropriate sales tax for your state for single issue orders. No sales tax for U.S. subscriptions. Canadian residents, add GST for subscriptions and single issues.)

_ Payment enclosed (U.S. check or money order only)
_ VISA _MC _AmEx _Discover Card #_____ Exp. Date _____

Signature _____ Day Phone _____
_ Bill Me (U.S. institutional orders only. Purchase order required.)

Purchase order # _____
         Federal Tax ID13559302   GST 89102 8052

Name _____

Address _____

_____

Phone _____ E-mail _____

For more information about Jossey-Bass, visit our Web site at www.josseybass.com

PROMOTION CODE ND03

issues in examination and negotiation of the political aspects of higher education, adult educators in K-12-focused colleges of education, literacy education, social welfare reform, professional organizations, and identity of the field.
ISBN 0-7879-5775-5

ACE90   Promoting Journal Writing in Adult Education
Leona M. English, Marie A. Gillen
Exploring the potential for personal growth and learning through journal writing for student and mentor alike, this volume aims to establish journal writing as an integral part of the teaching and learning process. Offers examples of how journal writing can be, and has been, integrated into educational areas as diverse as health education, higher education, education for women, and English as a Second Language.
ISBN 0-7879-5774-7

ACE89   The New Update on Adult Learning Theory
Sharan B. Merriam
A companion work to 1993's popular An Update on Adult Learning Theory, this issue examines the developments, research, and continuing scholarship in self-directed learning. Exploring context-based learning, informal and incidental learning, somatic learning, and narrative learning; the authors analyze recent additions to well-established theories and discuss the potential impact of today's cutting-edge approaches.
ISBN 0-7879-5773-9

ACE88   Strategic Use of Learning Technologies
Elizabeth J. Burge
The contributors draw on case examples to explore the advantages and disadvantages of three existing learning technologies—print, radio, and the Internet—and examine how a large urban university has carefully combined old and new technologies to provide a range of learner services tailored to its enormous and varied student body.
ISBN 0-7879-5426-8

ACE87   Team Teaching and Learning in Adult Education
Mary-Jane Eisen, Elizabeth J. Tisdell
The contributors show how team teaching can increase both organizational and individual learning in settings outside of a traditional classroom, for example, a recently deregulated public utility, a national literacy organization, and community-based settings such as Chicago's south side. They discuss how team teaching can be used in colleges and universities, describing strategies for administrators and teachers who want to integrate it into their curricula and classrooms.
ISBN 0-7879-5425-X

ACE86   Charting a Course for Continuing Professional Education: Reframing Professional Practice
Vivian W. Mott, Barbara J. Daley
This volume offers a resource to help practitioners examine and improve professional practice, and set new directions for the field of CPE across multiple professions. The contributors provide a brief review of the development of the field of CPE, analyze significant issues and trends that

are shaping and changing the field, and propose a vision of the future of CPE.
ISBN 0-7879-5424-1

ACE85 **Addressing the Spiritual Dimensions of Adult Learning: What Educators Can Do**
Leona M. English, Marie A. Gillen
The contributors discuss how mentoring, self-directed learning, and dialogue can be used to promote spiritual development, and advocate the learning covenant as a way of formalizing the sanctity of the bond between learners and educators. Drawing on examples from continuing professional education, community development, and health education, they show how a spiritual dimension has been integrated into adult education programs.
ISBN 0-7879-5364-4

ACE84 **An Update on Adult Development Theory: New Ways of Thinking About the Life Course**
M. Carolyn Clark, Rosemary J. Caffarella
This volume presents discussions of well-established theories and new perspectives on learning in adulthood. Knowles' andragogy, self-directed learning, Mezirow's perspective transformation, and several other models are assessed for their contribution to our understanding of adult learning. In addition, recent theoretical orientations, including consciousness and learning, situated cognition, critical theory, and feminist pedagogy, are discussed in terms of how each expands the knowledge base of adult learning.
ISBN 0-7879-1171-2

ACE83 **The Welfare-to-Work Challenge for Adult Literacy Educators**
Larry G. Martin, James C. Fisher
Welfare reform and workforce development legislation has had a dramatic impact on the funding, implementation, and evaluation of adult basic education and literacy programs. This issue provides a framework for literacy practitioners to better align their field with the demands of the Work First environment and to meet the pragmatic expectations of an extended list of stakeholders.
ISBN 0-7879-1170-4

ACE82 **Providing Culturally Relevant Adult Education: A Challenge for the Twenty-First Century**
Talmadge C. Guy
This issue offers more inclusive theories that focus on how learners construct meaning in a social and cultural context. Chapters identify ways that adult educators can work more effectively with racially, ethnically, and linguistically marginalized learners, and explore how adult education can be an effective tool for empowering learners to take control of their circumstances.
ISBN 0-7879-1167-4

ACE81 **Enhancing Creativity in Adult and Continuing Education: Innovative Approaches, Methods, and Ideas**
Paul Jay Edelson, Patricia L. Malone
The authors discuss innovations in a variety of continuing education settings, including the Harvard Institute for the Management of Lifelong

Education; a drug and alcohol prevention program; and a college degree program developed through the collaboration of the Bell Atlantic Corporation and a consortium of community colleges.
ISBN 0-7879-1169-0

ACE79   **The Power and Potential of Collaborative Learning Partnerships**
Iris M. Saltiel, Angela Sgroi, Ralph G. Brockett
This volume draws on examples of collaborative partnerships to explore the many ways collaboration can generate learning and knowledge. The contributors identify the factors that make for strong collaborative relationships, and they reveal how these partnerships actually help learners generate knowledge and insights well beyond what each brings to the learning situation.
ISBN 0-7879-9815-X

ACE78   **Adult Learning and the Internet**
Brad Cahoon
This volume explores the effects of the Internet on adult learning—both as that learning is facilitated through formal instruction and as it occurs spontaneously in the experiences of individuals and groups—and provides guidance to adult and continuing educators searching for ways to use the Internet effectively in their practice.
ISBN 0-7879-1166-6

ACE77   **Using Learning to Meet the Challenges of Older Adulthood**
James C. Fisher, Mary Alice Wolf
Combining theory and research in educational gerontology with the practice of older adult learning and education, this volume explores issues related to older adult education in academic and community settings. It is designed for educators and others concerned with the phenomenon of aging in America and with the continuing development of the field of educational gerontology.
ISBN 0-7879-1164-X

ACE75   **Assessing Adult Learning in Diverse Settings: Current Issues and Approaches**
Amy D. Rose, Meredyth A. Leahy
Examines assessment approaches analytically from different programmatic levels and looks at the implications of these differing approaches. Chapters discuss the implications of cultural differences as well as ideas about knowledge and knowing and the implications these ideas can have for both the participant and the program.
ISBN 0-7879-9840-0

ACE73   **Creating Practical Knowledge Through Action Research: Posing Problems, Solving Problems, and Improving Daily Practice**
B. Allan Quigley, Gary W. Kuhne
Outlines the process of action research step-by-step, provides a convenient project planner, and presents examples to show how action research yielded improvements in six different settings, including a hospital, a university, and a literacy education program.
ISBN 0-7879-9841-9

NEW DIRECTIONS
FOR ADULT AND CONTINUING EDUCATION
IS NOW AVAILABLE ONLINE AT WILEY INTERSCIENCE

What is Wiley InterScience?

Wiley InterScience is the dynamic online content service from John Wiley & Sons delivering the full text of over 300 leading scientific, technical, medical, and professional journals, plus major reference works, the acclaimed Current Protocols laboratory manuals, and even the full text of select Wiley print books online.

What are some special features of Wiley InterScience?

Wiley Interscience Alerts is a service that delivers table of contents via e-mail for any journal available on Wiley InterScience as soon as a new issue is published online.

EarlyView is Wiley's exclusive service presenting individual articles online as soon as they are ready, even before the release of the compiled print issue. These articles are complete, peer-reviewed, and citable.

CrossRef is the innovative multi-publisher reference linking system enabling readers to move seamlessly from a reference in a journal article to the cited publication, typically located on a different server and published by a different publisher.

How can I access Wiley InterScience?

Visit http://www.interscience.wiley.com.

Guest Users can browse Wiley InterScience for unrestricted access to journal tables of contents and article abstracts, or use the powerful search engine.

Registered Users are provided with a *Personal Home Page* to store and manage customized alerts, searches, and links to favorite journals and articles. Additionally, Registered Users can view free online sample issues and preview selected material from major reference works.

Licensed Customers are entitled to access full-text journal articles in PDF, with select journals also offering full-text HTML.

How do I become an Authorized User?

Authorized Users are individuals authorized by a paying Customer to have access to the journals in Wiley InterScience. For example, a university that subscribes to Wiley journals is considered to be the Customer. Faculty, staff and students authorized by the university to have access to those journals in Wiley InterScience are Authorized Users. Users should contact their library for information on which Wiley journals they have access to in Wiley InterScience.

United States Postal Service

Statement of Ownership, Management, and Circulation

1. Publication Title	2. Publication Number		3. Filing Date
New Directions For Adult And Continuing Education	0 1 9 5 — 2 2 4 2		9/26/02

4. Issue Frequency	5. Number of Issues Published Annually	6. Annual Subscription Price
Quarterly	4	$70.00 Individual $149.00 Institutic

7. Complete Mailing Address of Known Office of Publication (Not printer) (Street, city, county, state, and ZIP+4)

989 Market Street
San Francisco, CA 94103-1741
San Francisco County

Contact Person
Joe Schuman
Telephone
415 782 3232

8. Complete Mailing Address of Headquarters or General Business Office of Publisher (Not printer)

Same as above

9. Full Names and Complete Mailing Addresses of Publisher, Editor, and Managing Editor (Do not leave blank)

Publisher (Name and complete mailing address)

Jossey-Bass, A Wiley Company
Above Address

Editor (Name and complete mailing address)

Susan Imel
Ohio State University/Eric-Acve
1900 Kenny Road
Columbus, OH 43210-1090

Managing Editor (Name and complete mailing address)

None

10. Owner (Do not leave blank. If the publication is owned by a corporation, give the name and address of the corporation immediately followed by the names and addresses of all stockholders owning or holding 1 percent or more of the total amount of stock. If not owned by a corporation, give the names and addresses of the individual owners. If owned by a partnership or other unincorporated firm, give its name and address as well as those of each individual owner. If the publication is published by a nonprofit organization, give its name and address.)

Full Name	Complete Mailing Address
John Wiley & Sons Inc.	111 River Street Hoboken, NJ 07030

11. Known Bondholders, Mortgagees, and Other Security Holders Owning or Holding 1 Percent or More of Total Amount of Bonds, Mortgages, or Other Securities. If none, check box. ☐ None

Full Name	Complete Mailing Address
Same as Above	Same As Above

12. Tax Status (For completion by nonprofit organizations authorized to mail at nonprofit rates) (Check one)
The purpose, function, and nonprofit status of this organization and the exempt status for federal income tax purposes:
☐ Has Not Changed During Preceding 12 Months
☐ Has Changed During Preceding 12 Months (Publisher must submit explanation of change with this statement)

PS Form 3526, October 1999   (See Instructions on Reverse)

13. Publication Title	14. Issue Date for Circulation Data Below
New Directions For Adult And Continuing Education	Summer 2002

15. Extent and Nature of Circulation		Average No. Copies Each Issue During Preceding 12 Months	No. Copies of Single Issue Published Nearest to Filing Date
a. Total Number of Copies (Net press run)		1,550	1,519
b. Paid and/or Requested Circulation	(1) Paid/Requested Outside-County Mail Subscriptions Stated on Form 3541. (Include advertiser's proof and exchange copies)	676	666
	(2) Paid In-County Subscriptions Stated on Form 3541 (Include advertiser's proof and exchange copies)	0	0
	(3) Sales Through Dealers and Carriers, Street Vendors, Counter Sales, and Other Non-USPS Paid Distribution	0	0
	(4) Other Classes Mailed Through the USPS	0	0
c. Total Paid and/or Requested Circulation (Sum of 15b. (1), (2),(3),and (4)) ▲		676	666
d. Free Distribution by Mail (Samples, complimentary, and other free)	(1) Outside-County as Stated on Form 3541	0	0
	(2) In-County as Stated on Form 3541	0	0
	(3) Other Classes Mailed Through the USPS	1	1
e. Free Distribution Outside the Mail (Carriers or other means)		59	59
f. Total Free Distribution (Sum of 15d. and 15e.) ▲		60	60
g. Total Distribution (Sum of 15c. and 15f.) ▲		736	726
h. Copies not Distributed		814	793
i. Total (Sum of 15g. and h.) ▲		1,550	1,519
j. Percent Paid and/or Requested Circulation (15c. divided by 15g. times 100)		92%	92%

16. Publication of Statement of Ownership
☐ Publication required. Will be printed in the ___Winter 2002___ issue of this publication.   ☐ Publication not required.

17. Signature and Title of Editor, Publisher, Business Manager, or Owner

Susan E. Lewis   VP & Publisher - Periodicals

Date 9/26/02

I certify that all information furnished on this form is true and complete. I understand that anyone who furnishes false or misleading information on this form or who omits material or information requested on the form may be subject to criminal sanctions (including fines and imprisonment) and/or civil sanctions (including civil penalties).

Instructions to Publishers

1. Complete and file one copy of this form with your postmaster annually on or before October 1. Keep a copy of the completed form for your records.

2. In cases where the stockholder or security holder is a trustee, include in items 10 and 11 the name of the person or corporation for whom the trustee is acting. Also include the names and addresses of individuals who are stockholders who own or hold 1 percent or more of the total amount of bonds, mortgages, or other securities of the publishing corporation. In item 11, if none, check the box. Use blank sheets if more space is required.

3. Be sure to furnish all circulation information called for in item 15. Free circulation must be shown in items 15d, e, and f.

4. Item 15h., Copies not Distributed, must include (1) newsstand copies originally stated on Form 3541, and returned to the publisher, (2) estimated returns from news agents, and (3), copies for office use, leftovers, spoiled, and all other copies not distributed.

5. If the publication had Periodicals authorization as a general or requester publication, this Statement of Ownership, Management, and Circulation must be published; it must be printed in any issue in October or, if the publication is not published during October, the first issue printed after October.

6. In item 16, indicate the date of the issue in which this Statement of Ownership will be published.

7. Item 17 must be signed.

Failure to file or publish a statement of ownership may lead to suspension of Periodicals authorization.

PS Form 3526, October 1999 (Reverse)